Results Not Receipts

Results Not Receipts

Counting the Right Things in Aid and Corruption

Charles Kenny

CENTER FOR GLOBAL DEVELOPMENT
Washington, D.C.

Copyright © 2017
CENTER FOR GLOBAL DEVELOPMENT
2055 L St. NW
Washington DC 20036
www.cgdev.org

Library of Congress Cataloging-in-Publication data
Names: Kenny, Charles, author.
Title: Results not receipts : counting the right things in aid and corruption / by Charles Kenny.
Description: Washington, DC : Center For Global Development, [2017] |
   Includes bibliographical references and index.
Identifiers: LCCN 2017005587 | ISBN 9781933286976 (pbk.)
Subjects: LCSH: Economic assistance—Developing countries. | Corrup-
   tion—Developing countries. | Economic development—Developing
   countries.
Classification: LCC HC60 .K4335 2017 | DDC 338.9109172/4—dc23 LC
   record available at https://lccn.loc.gov/2017005587

Contents

Preface

Governance and corruption remain at the heart of discussions around global development. The idea that "institutions rule" in explaining long-term development outcomes has endured as a consensus since the second half of the 1990s. Corruption in particular was singled out as a significant barrier to development by former World Bank president James Wolfensohn in a 1996 speech when he labeled it a cancer. It is still a preoccupation of aid agencies worldwide, reflected in aid allocation formulae, projects supporting reform of government operations, procurement and financial management regimes, and internal audit and oversight bodies.

It is right that corruption is a concern of aid agencies—millions of those whom they are dedicated to assisting are forced to pay bribes each year for essential services or to avoid arbitrary arrest. Many billions of dollars are lost each year to contractors who pay bureaucrats to look the other way as they deliver shoddy construction projects and substandard supplies at inflated prices. Corruption at the highest levels of government can skew the whole course of development.

At the same time, the discussion of corruption response should take place in the context of immense recent progress in developing countries; governance failures are serious issues in developed and developing countries alike, but clearly not insurmountable challenges to economic growth, poverty reduction, and improved health and well-being. That suggests the issue of corruption should not be used as an excuse to deny assistance, nor to add donor controls and bureaucracy that may look like a response but in practice turn out to be of little impact.

Results Not Receipts argues the donor response to corruption should rest on the same principles that apply to all effective aid: it should be evidence-based and designed to maximize development impact. This book suggests that the current approaches by donors to dealing with corruption are sometimes based on weak evidence of effectiveness and a lack of focus on outcomes. Because we cannot accurately measure most forms of corruption, we should measure the impact and utility of corruption-fighting tools on the basis of outcomes—electricity delivered, students taught, children vaccinated. And results-based payments are a powerful anticorruption tool because outcomes delivered at a competitive price leave little scope for the rents that fuel malfeasance.

In championing a focus on results, this book fits into a broader stream of CGD work including Cash on Delivery Aid and development impact bonds. On aid effectiveness, the Center created the Quality of Official Development Assistance, or QuODA, which scored development agencies on features including efficiency, reduced institutional burden to recipients, and greater transparency that are among the concerns of *Results Not Receipts*. More broadly, the Center has pushed for transparency and reform around government contracting, taxation, and trade, which Charles Kenny highlights as some of the more effective tools for reducing the development impact of corruption.

I hope this book helps to spark renewed debate in donor agencies about approaches to reduce the impact of corruption on delivering effective aid and development.

Masood Ahmed
PRESIDENT
CENTER FOR GLOBAL DEVELOPMENT

Acknowledgments

Some of the material presented here has appeared in Center for Global Development (CGD) and World Bank working papers (with Bill Savedoff, Casey Dunning, Jonathan Karver, Maria Musatova, and Tina Soreide) and in articles in *Utilities Policy*, the *Journal of Development Studies*, the *ICE Journal*, *Governance*, *Foreign Policy*, *Businessweek*, and *Bloomberg*. Thanks to coauthors, editors, and reviewers for their suggestions, contributions, and time. Thank you for excellent research assistance to Dev Patel, Ben Crisman, Maria Cecilia Ramirez, Jonathan Karver, and Sarah Dykstra.

My considerable gratitude goes to Bill Savedoff for detailed and very helpful comments on a first draft. Thanks for comments on a second draft to Jonah Busch, Alan Hudson, Johannes Tonn, Tina Søreide, Brad Parks, Maya Forstater, David McNair, Rupert Simons, Milford Bateman, Bruce Murray, Frank Vogl, Andrew Marshall, and Finn Heinrich and the team at Transparency International. Duncan Green provided reactions on his blog and so did a number of commenters there, including Cheyanne Scharbatke-Church, Anders Ostman, and Allan Moolman. In addition, there were commenters on my CGD blog post that included the draft: Narayan Manandhar, Kenneth Schofield, Francisco Mejia, Alice Evans, Hans Gutbrod, Felipe Manteiga, John Heilbrunn, Heather Marquette, Brian Levy, and Orin Levine. I presented the draft at the UK Department for International Development and benefited from reactions from Jonathan

Hargreaves, Phil Mason, and other colleagues. Thanks for insightful official review comments from Stefan Dercon as well as participants at the CGD review meeting for the book. Finally, thanks to John Osterman, Emily Schabacker, and Rajesh Mirchandani for helpful suggestions on flow and copyediting. The book is now, I hope, stronger in tone, style, and substance thanks to their many valuable insights and reactions. Any tone-deaf and incoherent errors that remain are all too clearly mine.

1

The Two Problems of Corruption and Poor Governance

After the invasion of Afghanistan in late 2001, the U.S. Agency for International Development (USAID) developed a program to provide basic health care to the population, which languished at the bottom of global rankings of child survival and maternal health. The U.S. aid agency supported the Afghan Ministry of Public Health in delivering a basic package of health care to 90 percent of the country at a cost of $4.50 per person per year, largely through contracts with nongovernmental service providers. The program focused on measureable results, and USAID commissioned an independent evaluation that found that vaccination rates and the provision of services such as family planning shot up between 2004 and 2010. Partly as a result, from 2004 to 2010 Afghanistan experienced the most rapid increase in life expectancy worldwide, from 42 to 62 years. This increase was driven by a drop in child mortality that each year kept alive 100,000 children who previously would have died.

But accounting standards at the Ministry of Public Health troubled one of the oversight bodies that monitors USAID's work: the U.S. Special Inspector General for Afghanistan Reconstruction (SIGAR). SIGAR's mission is to "promote economy and efficiency of U.S.-funded reconstruction programs in Afghanistan and to detect and deter fraud, waste, and abuse."

1

It called for the health program to be suspended because of "financial management deficiencies" at the ministry.[1]

In spite of these claims, SIGAR's investigation into the USAID health care delivery program found no evidence of corruption, and there was no argument about its success.[2] All the results were fantastic, but according to the U.S. government the health program's receipts were not in order, and thus the program was condemned. This case is far from an isolated incident, and illustrates a growing problem: The focus on corruption as a barrier to development progress has led donor agencies to make policy and institutional changes that are damaging the potential for aid to deliver development. This book examines ways to fix that problem.

Why Isn't Development Working?

A focus on corruption as a factor in development has sharpened over the past two decades, with the launch of Transparency International in 1993, the 1997 Organization for Economic Cooperation and Development (OECD) Convention on Combating Bribery of Foreign Public Officials in International Business Transactions, and the 2003 United Nations Convention against Corruption. The concern has engulfed donors as well. In 1996, World Bank president James Wolfensohn gave a celebrated speech on "the cancer of corruption" and created an internal unit to track fraud and corruption in the organization's projects. European donors created the U4 Anti-Corruption Resource Center and ramped up spending on corruption and governance programs. And institutions such as the World Bank and the U.S. Millennium Challenge Corporation (MCC) have added measures of institutional weakness or corruption risk to their financial allocation formulas.

In development thinking, weak governance and corruption are seen primarily as challenges to the efficient delivery of outcomes such as health, income growth, education, infrastructure, and a thriving private sector. There is no doubt that failures of governance and corruption do present such challenges. The examples are legion—from crumbling schools and absent teachers to bribe-happy police officers, from capriciously enforced

---

1 Sandefur (2013).
2 Sandefur (2013).

regulation all the way to kleptocracy on a scale large enough to drain treasuries. But there is a second problem of corruption in development, and it is the donors' response to the (perceived) threat. The belief that weak governance is the major problem of development, and the conclusion that the problem is intractable, justifies aid fatigue—a resigned sense that "it's broke, and we can't fix it." Concern with weak governance and the risk of malfeasance is the primary justification for donors to heavily interfere with or even directly select, design, and manage projects from distant donor capitals, making such projects slow, expensive, and (often) of limited impact. Perhaps more important, countries that are perceived as corrupt simply attract less foreign investment and trade.

If corruption really were an insurmountable stumbling block to delivering development, and if we really knew which countries or states were particularly corrupt, this second problem of corruption would not be a bug of the system; it would be a feature. Tight control (if it worked) and aid fatigue (if it did not) would be a logical response. But there is no compelling evidence that weak governance is a barrier to all development progress or effective aid programs, and donors know considerably less than one might think about which countries (or sectors or activities) are weakly governed or particularly corrupt. As a result, anticorruption approaches can do more harm than good. And although in the short term it may be useful for donors to frame the development discussion around their recipients' failures, in the long term such a negative perspective is bad for recipients and donors alike. Saying that a country is poor because it is corrupt, and that it is corrupt because of slow-changing institutions, is a way of avoiding the moral responsibility to act.

As important, it is not even clear that external anticorruption approaches reduce corruption. Donors have treated corruption as an issue that they can measure and improve, and from which they can insulate (or ring-fence) their projects at acceptable costs. They focus on countering corruption in their own projects by monitoring receipts, and they direct funds based on perceptions of corruption. But aid outcomes are not significantly determined by donor procurement oversight, nor are they derailed by the kind of activities that corruption indicators appear to reflect. Moreover, aid-financed anticorruption efforts do not appear to do much to change those corruption indicators.

It is time for donor agencies to fundamentally rethink their anticorruption approaches. Rather than trying to measure the dimensions of the black box of corruption and change its internal dynamics, this book suggests that donors should focus instead on shrinking the box by minimizing the impact that corruption can have on aid outcomes. If an aid project produces good results at a fair price, the rents that drive corruption will be reduced.

And although governance and probity are both important to development outcomes, the ideology of institutional determinism—that poor, historically rooted institutions necessarily lead to poor development—has weak empirical roots, and the application of this ideology to development policy relies on even weaker evidence. Approaches including the MCC's "hard hurdle," which excludes countries from assistance on the basis of perceived corruption, alongside tighter procurement oversight by multilateral agencies, not only lack a solid rationale but also carry considerable costs. Donor agencies have a role in governance and anticorruption efforts, but corruption is but one of many barriers to development, and the role of outsiders in the process is limited, context-specific, and dependent on many unknowns.

This book will cover what is known about governance, corruption, and development, and what that knowledge means for aid policy. It will look at the disconnect between the kind of corruption that concerns people in developing and rich countries alike and the corruption that donors focus on. It will evaluate the quality of existing measures of corruption; lay out the case against institutional determinism; explore what is known about how to improve institutions and, in particular, the role for outsiders in that process; and finally make some policy conclusions regarding development practice in bodies such as the World Bank and bilateral development agencies. It will then conclude by examining what the broader context for aid suggests about the declining relevance of the aid project and related project-level anticorruption approaches, regardless of the questionable efficacy of these approaches.

The Costs of Weak Governance and Corruption

These concerns aside, corruption is a real and significant challenge to development, and should be an issue of donor focus. It is possible to distinguish corruption by type of gain (power, money, position, goods or services), by method of corruption (bribery, embezzlement, future employment) or by the target influenced (laws and regulatory design, legal or regulatory application, procurements, hiring decisions, distribution of resources or services), but in the spirit of this book's focus on results, the following sections address some of the varied impacts of corruption.

Leakage and Stealing

There is a lot of bribe-paying in the world. According to Transparency International's Global Corruption Barometer, one-half or more of its respondents in the poorest countries report paying a bribe. The comparable number in most rich countries is less than 10 percent (see figure 1-1). Every year, as many as 1.6 billion people pay bribes for government services, and about one-third of people worldwide who deal with the police report having paid a bribe.[3] Within countries, corruption is frequently regressive; poor people are made to bribe with greater regularity, often for access to services that should be free.[4] Firms bribe as well, of course: the global total value of bribe payments may be as high as 2 percent of global gross domestic product (GDP).[5]

In some cases, the bribes are a pure shakedown—government officials stealing from citizens. In other cases, bribes help citizens steal from the government. For example, in Bangladesh and Orissa, India, in the mid-2000s, only around 55 percent of generated power was paid for. The rest was lost to technical and commercial losses. Of this, perhaps 15 to 18 percent of the losses were accounted for by true technical losses, suggesting that illegal connections or underbilling accounted for as much as 30 percent of generated power.[6] Much of that loss was facilitated by bribe payments to electricity workers.

Officials also steal from the government. Public-expenditure tracking surveys, which track the flow of resources through the layers of government bureaucracy, have found significant leakage of funds—between 30 and 76 percent of nonwage funds designated for primary schools in African countries, for example. Some, perhaps most, of these losses were from redirection of resources rather than outright theft, but these find-

---

3 Rose (2015).

4 Transparency International (2015).

5 International Monetary Fund (2016).

6 Gulati and Rao (2006). Similarly, Davis (2004) suggests that 35 percent of total water flows in India come from unaccounted-for water.

Figure 1-1. Bribery Is More Common in Poor Countries

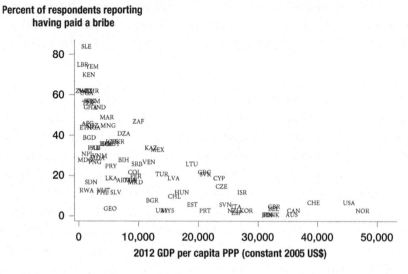

Source: Transparency International Global Corruption Barometer and World Bank World Development Indicators

ings nonetheless suggest the potential scale of the problem of official theft. Government employees can also "steal" from the state by failing to perform their duties. Eleven percent of teachers are absent from school on the average day in Peru, 16 percent are absent in Bangladesh, 25 percent in India, and 27 percent in Uganda. In unannounced visits to schools in Andhra Pradesh in India, the chance that a teacher—a civil servant, and therefore a government employee—was actually in a class and actively engaged in teaching during the school day was 28 percent.[7]

Increased Price of Investment

Rampant bribery and calculated theft have significant knock-on effects in affected regions and countries. Not least, they increase the cost of government investment. Using data on World Bank–financed road projects, it is possible to analyze the average costs per square meter for a standard

---

7 Reinikka and Svensson (2002).

road reconstruction assignment.[8] Costs for road rehabilitation are higher in countries where the average bribe paid for government contracts (as reported in World Bank Enterprise Surveys) is larger. The average cost paid per square meter for rehabilitation of a two-lane highway across 18 countries for which there are good data was $36. In countries where the average bribe for a government contract was reported to be below 2 percent of the contract value, this cost was $30. For countries where bribes for government contracts were reported to be larger than 2 percent of their value, the average cost per square meter of road rehabilitated was $46.[9]

Decreased Returns on Investment

Weak governance and corruption can also reduce the quality of investment. The World Bank Integrity Department's review of Bank-financed projects in India's health sector provides some examples of such poor-quality work. To assess a health project in Orissa, civil engineers visited 55 project hospitals and found that 93 percent of them had problems such as uninitiated or incomplete work; severely leaking roofs; crumbling ceilings; molding walls; and nonfunctional water, sewage, or electrical systems financed under the project. Yet the construction management consultants who supervised the work certified that 38 of these hospitals were complete and in line with project specifications, and in February 2006 the Orissa Department of Health and Family Welfare reported that work at 45 of them was complete.[10]

Low-quality construction related to corruption can reduce the longevity of new infrastructure by as much as one-half or more. One estimate is that every dollar's worth of materials skimped in road projects to finance corrupt payments reduces the economic benefit of the road by $3.41 as a result of degraded quality and shortened lifespan.[11]

---

8 This analysis is for a two-lane road between 6 and 8 meters wide with a bituminous surface, for countries with four or more estimates based on individual project data. Data are drawn from the World Bank's Road Cost Knowledge System (ROCKS) database, www.worldbank.org/transport/roads/rd_tools/rocks_main.htm.

9 Kenny (2009).

10 Olken (2007).

11 Ibid.

Reduced Quality of Regulation

Alongside publicly funded infrastructure, private infrastructure projects can be seriously and negatively impacted by the deleterious effects that corruption and poor governance have on regulation. Buildings in developing countries often collapse as the result of substandard construction.[12] In 1999, more than half of all buildings in Turkey failed to comply with construction regulations, even though 98 percent of the country's population lives in earthquake-prone zones.[13] One result of this regulatory evasion is massive loss of life: in 1999, 11,000 people died as a result of shoddy construction when an earthquake struck near Istanbul. In the 2010 Haitian earthquake, building collapses claimed numerous lives because existing building codes had not been enforced.[14] Bribery and the "theft of time" by regulatory employees may well have been two of the factors behind these tragedies.

In the developing world, politicians and bureaucrats often use—and design—regulations specifically to extract bribes or other favors rather than to actually make things safer, more sustainable, or more efficient. Mary Hallward-Driemeier of the World Bank and Lant Pritchett of Harvard's Kennedy School examined data on the length of time it should take for firms to legally obtain a construction permit and the time that firms reported actually having spent to get those permits across countries. There was almost no relationship at all between the measures. In Brazil, for example, the actual time taken to get a construction permit in reality averages 85 days. If all regulations had been followed to the letter, it would take 411 days to receive the same permit.[15]

Looking across countries, going from an official time requirement of 77 days to 601 days increases the *actual* time taken to get a license by the firms whose requests were granted fastest by a mere three days. For disfavored firms—those that may not have good connections or are unwilling to bribe the necessary people—it is a different story: for them, the time taken to get a permit climbs by 130 days. And World Bank analysis suggests that countries with particularly onerous official licensing processes are also those where firms report more serious problems with corruption.[16]

---

12 Polgreen and Khwaja (2010).
13 Bohlen (1999).
14 Kenny (2011).
15 Hallward-Driemeier and Pritchett (2011).
16 Madani and Licetti (2010).

At its extreme, the regulatory apparatus of the state can be bent to the considerable benefit of a very small coterie. Enterprises with direct ownership links to disgraced Tunisian president Ben Ali accounted for about 3 percent of Tunisia's private-sector output but 20 percent of profits. The sectors in which Ben Ali firms were active were significantly more likely to be subject to prior government authorization and foreign direct investment (FDI) restrictions. In those sectors, only the Ben Ali firms made outsize profits, suggesting that regulatory capture was the reason for the family's business success.[17]

Public Attitudes to Aid in the West

With all of this evidence that corruption is a real and pervasive issue in developing countries, it should not be surprising that corruption is a big concern for citizens in donor countries when they think about overseas development assistance. But many people in the rich world go further: they have attitudes toward developing countries that would make Rudyard Kipling, poet propagandist for empire, proud. Public opinion in Europe and the United States appears to be that developing-country governments are simply useless, and the citizens of developing countries are helpless in the face of kleptocracy.

A recent survey by InterMedia looked at popular attitudes toward international development in France, Germany, the United Kingdom, and the United States, among others.[18] The good news is that a lot of people in Europe and America care about global development. Between 31 percent (United States) and 50 percent (United Kingdom) of the four rich-country populations surveyed are interested in international development or global health issues and have participated in social or political engagement (from donating or volunteering through blogging or tweeting) in the past six months. The report calls them "interested citizens." But the bad news is the widespread belief that only the rich world can save poor countries. When asked who was primarily responsible for addressing challenges

---

17 Rijkers, Freund, and Nucifora (2014).

18 InterMedia, n.d., "Building Support for International Development: A New Inter-Media Research Report," www.intermedia.org/building-support-for-international-development-a-new-intermedia-research-report/.

in developing countries, many of these interested citizens in rich countries suggested outsiders were primarily responsible. In France, 52 percent felt that the primary responsibility fell to rich-world governments and international organizations, compared to only 26 percent for governments in the developing world. In the United Kingdom the same shares were 27 percent and 50 percent. In the United States each view had an equal 39 percent support.

What underlies the widespread belief that only the rich world can save poor countries is the sense that people and governments in the developing world are completely useless at helping themselves. A 2011 review in the United Kingdom suggests that the dominant image of developing countries remains "malnutrition and pot-bellied young children desperate for help with flies on their faces."[19] Perhaps this image problem is not surprising when well-intentioned efforts to mobilize support for famine relief or prosecution of war criminals in Africa tend to emphasize the worst of the continent and play up the role of outsiders in bringing change.

Regarding aid, according to the abovementioned British review there is close to "a universal feeling that efforts have long been made to combat poverty in places like Africa and yet little has changed." The common explanation for this impression, according to InterMedia, is corrupted aid. Only between 16 percent (in France) and 29 percent (in the United Kingdom) of interested citizens in rich countries disagreed with the statement that "most financial aid to developing countries [is] wasted." Between 44 percent (in the United States) and 66 percent (France) agreed.

Set "interested citizens" aside, and the opinion that aid is wasted is even stronger among the general population. The median survey respondent in the United States thinks that 60 percent of aid ends up in the hands of corrupt officials. It is no surprise that this perspective leads to aid fatigue. Between September 2008 and February 2010, the percentage of people in the United Kingdom suggesting that corruption in poor-country governments makes it pointless to give money climbed from 44 percent to 57 percent, while support for increased government action to reduce

---

19 Darnton and Kirk (2011, p. 23).

global poverty slipped from 49 percent to 35 percent. And more than half of respondents suggested that the single most important reason for why poor countries are poor is because of corrupt governments.[20]

Concern with corruption unites popular distrust of government across the political spectrum, from those who think that governments are in hock to big business to those who think that government is simply a license to print money for bureaucrats and politicians. This distrust is a big problem because no country has become wealthy without a large government, one involved in a huge range of regulatory, investment, and spending roles. No high-income member of the OECD club of rich countries has general government spending lower than 31 percent of GDP, according to the OECD's own data. South Korea has the lowest level, and it still spends around $10,000 per person per year on government services and investment.[21] By pandering to those who distrust government in the West, donors' obsessive focus on corruption helps to hobble governments in the developing world, with dire consequences for aid levels and effectiveness as well as broader development progress.

At one time, the common explanation for why poor countries were poor was because they lacked financing and resources. Now, all too many appear to believe that the cause of this poverty is the moral failings of the people in those countries—the same reasoning used to justify cuts to domestic social safety nets, freeing countries of any obligation to help their own poor. When it comes to aiding poor countries abroad, the opinion that "they are corrupt" is a reasonable excuse for apathy.

The Aid Agency Response to Corruption

Aid agencies have responded to the real evidence of corruption alongside popular concerns with corruption in donor programs with tough talk. World Bank president Jim Kim recently declared that "in the developing world, corruption is public enemy number one," and that "we will never

---

20 Skelly, Chalisey, and Pierson (2010).

21 Data from OECD, "General Government Spending," https://data.oecd.org/gga/gen eral-government-spending.htm.

tolerate corruption."[22] But agencies also have responded by centralizing processes, running projects out of donor capitals with little involvement of beneficiary governments or people.

Former USAID administrator Andrew Natsios lists the web of oversight and control institutions that ensure USAID staff spend most of their time monitoring compliance:

> The Offices of the Inspectors General; the Office of Management and Budget; the Government Accountability Office; the Office of the Director of Foreign Assistance in the State Department; the Special Inspector General for Iraq Reconstruction and the Special Inspector General for Afghanistan Reconstruction; a set of voluminous federal law, such as the Federal Acquisition Regulations—the infamous 1,977-page FAR—that governs all federal contracts for all federal departments, including USAID; [the Defense Department's] regulatory control over all overhead rates for all federal contractors and grantees, including USAID; Congressional oversight committees; and the 450-page Foreign Assistance Act of 1961, among many others.

Natsios suggests that this network of regulatory oversight, which he labels "the counter-bureaucracy," lies behind donor countries' preference for working with large Washington-based contractors (who understand all of these regulations), rather than with recipient-country or small providers. He also reports that as many as one-third of all USAID staff are hired explicitly to fulfill compliance duties at the agency.[23]

USAID's Afghan health project, discussed at the start of this chapter, is just one example of the impact that the concern over controls can have on a development project. Aid to Haiti after the devastating 2010 earthquake is another. Because of low faith in the government's fiduciary capacity, only 1 percent of 2010–11 aid flows to Haiti went through the government while hundreds of millions went to nongovernmental organizations (NGOs)

---

22 World Bank, "Corruption Is 'Public Enemy Number One' in Developing Countries, Says World Bank Group President Kim," December 19, 2013, www.worldbank.org/en/news/press-release/2013/12/19/corruption-developing-countries-world-bank-group-president-kim.

23 Natsios (2010).

and contractors. In 2010 and 2011 combined, the Haitian government received about $23 million in aid, an amount less than what the U.S. government contracted with Chemonics International, Lakeshore Engineering Services, Development Alternatives Inc., PAE Government Systems, and Management Sciences for Health for their work in Haiti. This model may have ensured elegant accounting records regarding every penny spent, but it appears to have done less when it came to rapid recovery in Haiti itself. Furthermore, it is worth noting how much these centralized approaches contradict the internationally agreed Paris Principles on aid effectiveness: that aid that is "owned" by recipient countries and runs through government budgets is likely to be more effective.[24]

Concerns over receipts and the resulting pressure to centralize aid spending has spread through a number of aid agencies. For example, about one-fifth of global bilateral aid is delivered through NGOs, nearly all of whom are headquartered in donor countries.[25] Much of the rest comes through private firms based in those same countries. By comparison, as of 2014, general budget support to recipient countries accounted for less than 1 percent of bilateral aid flows according to OECD data. For most donor agencies, moreover, receipt-tracking has become a larger endeavor than results-tracking. The World Bank spends considerably more each year on procurement and financial management specialists and investigators looking for fraud and corruption than it does on evaluations of whether its projects have achieved their intended outcomes for improving wealth, health, and well-being.[26] The focus on receipts makes for bureaucratically costly aid that achieves less.

Corruption concerns have also been used to channel aid flows. The World Bank's "Country Policy and Institutional Assessment," which includes a subjective staff assessment of corruption levels, helps determine the institution's level of low-interest lending to poorer countries. Similarly, the MCC notes that control of corruption is one of its highest priorities.[27] As mentioned above, it uses a "hard hurdle" in its selection procedure that requires a country to score above the median of its income group on the

---

24 See OECD, n.d., "Paris Declaration and Accra Agenda for Action," www.oecd.org/dac/effectiveness/parisdeclarationandaccraagendaforaction.htm.

25 OECD (2013).

26 Kenny and Savedoff (2013).

27 Millennium Challenge Corporation (2007, p. 2).

control of corruption component of the World Bank's Worldwide Governance Indicators: "The inclusion of the Control of Corruption indicator as a hard hurdle is tied directly to MCC's mission to pursue economic growth and poverty reduction. Economics literature shows the importance of controlling corruption for economic growth and poverty reduction," the MCC explains. It further justifies tying eligibility for compact assistance to performance on the control of corruption indicator by noting that "if donors are going to provide more assistance, recipient countries need to provide greater accountability and deliver results."[28] Although the empirical evidence underlying the MCC's claims is fragile at best, the system remains in place.

The corruption-fighting industrial complex that donor countries have created has every incentive to sacrifice development outcomes and efficiency to the quixotic search for accounting purity in fragile states. Tina Søreide from the Chr. Michelsen Center suggests that as NGOs get more funding for anticorruption work, they are increasingly likely to point at corruption: "[T]he whole development community is 'guilty' of signaling (too?) high levels of corruption."[29] As Søreide also points out, there are negative effects of the focus on corruption beyond the aid industry. Global measures like Transparency International's perception indicators label some countries as extremely corrupt, a statement that depresses a range of engagement between North and South such as trade, travel, and private investment. Who would think of setting up a factory in a region supposedly run by crooks?[30] For those who do engage, the very label of corruption increases the temptation to engage in wrongdoing: considerable experimental evidence suggests that firm executives who are acting in what they believe is a "culture of corruption" have a less psychologically demanding time deciding to bribe.[31]

The din of complaint and concern about corruption by rich-country politicians and leaders of multilateral institutions also drowns out softer

---

28 Ibid.

29 Søreide (2014).

30 Brouthers, Gao, and McNicol (2008); and Habib and Zurawicki (2002).

31 See also Corbacho and others (2016). Søreide (2009) notes that middlemen, agents, and legal firms that offer "facilitation" services and arm's-length relationships with government officials have a positive incentive to suggest that most firms pay bribes or that local officials are incompetent or corrupt. In fact, they have the incentive to create that situation. This might make the risk-averse strategy be the strategy to bribe.

rhetoric about more obscene misdeeds. There is a perhaps uncomfortable irony that donors' statements and actions on steering a contract or taking a bribe are far more strident than on the forced genital mutilation of women, the imprisonment of protestors, or the torture of political opponents. Seen in this light, it might appear that corruption is a cancer to be fought with all possible means while torture and intimidation are minor misfortunes that the polite do not dwell upon.

Toward a New Vision

Thankfully, the model of hopeless peoples under kleptocratic and incompetent leadership is at best a partial view of the developing world. Corruption and weak governance are all too common, but the quality of life across the planet is better than it has ever been. Incomes are rising, mortality is falling, education rates are climbing, and the number of electoral democracies is increasing. The proportion of people living on less than $1.25 a day worldwide has far more than halved since 1990. In Africa, eight economies in the region doubled in size over the course of the most recent decade. Furthermore, the overwhelming reason for all of this change is not charitable giving by the people and governments of rich countries, it is the efforts of the people and—it is important to emphasize—*governments* of the developing world. Given how small aid flows are compared to the economic size of most countries that receive it, development assistance has had an outsize impact. Successes such as the eradication of smallpox and rinderpest and the elimination of polio from Africa depended crucially on aid, and there is growing evidence that aid is a force for economic growth as well.[32] Nonetheless, such assistance accounts for an average of about 1 percent of the GDP of recipient countries.[33] Assume for the sake of argument that aid is a tool for development 10 times more powerful than a recipient country's domestic resources—that would still mean the development story is 90 percent about the domestic activities of the developing world, alongside trade, investment, and migration, rather than aid.

These facts highlight that the strict anticorruption approach to aid is nested in a broader misunderstanding of the role of foreign assistance in

---

32 Galiani and others (2014).
33 Kenny (2012).

development. Aid is no longer about financing foreign exchange and major parts of national investment programs. The traditional model for aid is dated in all but a few small, poor economies and postconflict states. A new model for aid is needed, one that emphasizes results over receipts. That model would involve tracking outcomes of projects and, where possible, paying recipients on the basis of those outcomes. Such a model provides the right incentives for development projects to succeed and minimizes the ability of corruption to derail them—but it does so by design rather than by constant oversight.

The evidence on corruption, aid, and development also implies lessons for how aid agencies and NGOs frame the narrative on what they do: beyond emphasizing success over control when discussing developing countries, they should emphasize agency over helplessness. If they focus on failure and stagnation in Africa or South Asia, highlight corruption, and suggest that poor people will make improvements only with the help of the rich, they reinforce the toxic narrative of failure. Donors should care about corruption—it is a serious tax on development progress that can hit the poorest hardest—but they should respond with approaches that work to deliver development rather than hinder it.

The following chapters make the case against the assumptions that underlie the current donor consensus on corruption and aid. Chapter 2 questions the common measures of corruption, specifically looking at the disconnect between the popular concern with corruption and survey evidence of bribe payments and "expert perceptions" indexes. Expert perceptions appear to be biased and inaccurate measures of both bribery levels and popular concern about corruption; it is very unclear what they actually measure. Even survey estimates of bribery appear uncertain, but they do suggest that any one measure of national corruption is likely to hide considerable variations within countries. The existing direct corruption measures are not good enough to be used for decisionmaking or determining what works. We can measure a range of outcomes, however, and these outcome measurements are linked to a country's success at tackling corruption.

Chapter 3 challenges a model of development that suggests that weak governance and corruption are slow-changing, insurmountable barriers to development progress. Corruption, at least as it is usually measured, is an important factor in development outcomes, but it is not the ultimate arbiter of future development success. Consequently, anticorruption efforts can do more harm than good.

Chapter 4 turns to responses, focusing on transparency and results measurement as key tools to improve outcomes at the country level. Chapter 5 discusses the weak empirical basis for current donor approaches to anticorruption and calls again for a focus on transparency and outcomes. Finally, chapter 6 directly addresses supporters of the current approach to corruption and suggests that the inconvenient truths that this book has outlined emphasize the need to focus on results, not receipts.

Countries are (largely) responsible for their own destiny, and the results of the past 15 years suggest that they can make remarkable, at times historically unprecedented, progress on development outcomes. Donors that reinforce misinformed domestic popular perceptions that the developing world is a corrupt and hopeless mess do themselves and developing countries no favors. It is time for a new approach.

2
Measuring What Wants to Be Hidden

Attempts to measure corruption have proliferated over the past two decades, not least with the launch of Transparency International's Corruption Perceptions Index (CPI) and the rollout of enterprise and consumer surveys that include questions on the extent of informal payments for licenses, government services, and contracts. These corruption metrics have been used to determine aid allocations (for the U.S. Millennium Challenge Corporation, for example) and guide approaches to reform.

Such exercises are useful only if the measures reasonably reflect an underlying reality of corruption. But defining corruption is surprisingly difficult. Like pornography, most people think that they know corruption when they see it—but in many cases, different people see different things and draw different conclusions accordingly. If individual acts of corruption are difficult to label, then it is likely that perceptions of a general state of national corruption will be even more problematic.

If the evaluator's chosen measure of corruption is reported petty bribery, then developing countries are considerably more corrupt than rich countries. According to Transparency International surveys, 10 percent of Americans and 6 percent of Britons report having been asked to pay a bribe. Compare those respondent figures with 22 percent in Turkey; 33 percent in Pakistan; or more than 50 percent in countries such as Senegal, Ghana, and the Democratic Republic of the Congo.[1] In global surveys of firms that ask how often firms like theirs make side payments for anything from avoiding taxes to winning a government contract, there is a strong pattern: the poorer the country, the more likely firms are to make such payments. If the measure of corruption is based on "expert perceptions"—the opinion of international consultants and business advisory services—once again poor countries are considerably more corrupt than rich countries. However, these perceptions may simply reflect the fact that these measures are strongly correlated with petty bribe payments. They appear to do a poorer job of reflecting other indicators of corruption.

Survey measures of bribery may be considerably more reliable than perception indicators, but they are still subject to systemic bias and error, which make it difficult to measure the scale of the problem. Survey evidence also suggests that corruption—or at least the level of bribe payments—varies considerably within countries by sector, activity, and location, meaning that any single country-level measure would considerably oversimplify a complicated reality. Again, different types of corruption can be more or less harmful, which suggests that specific measures, such as bribes as a percentage of contract values, may be poor proxies for the development impact of corruption. Finally, people worldwide appear to be concerned about corruption in a far broader sense of the term than that captured by bribe payments. They are worried about a system stacked against the common man. They appear to believe that corruption in this broader sense is as much a feature of rich countries as poor ones. And they may have a point: on most measures of outcomes that might reflect "elite capture"—a local elite diverting resources meant for the broader population to themselves—rich countries look as bad as poor ones.

If the existing measures of corruption are so weak, how can donor and recipient countries know what works to stop it? The answer is to look at the very development outcomes that corruption purportedly affects: poor, inefficient government services with limited reach. Evaluators have far better measures of the efficiency, quality, and extent of service provision and the extent of development than those of corruption because it is much harder to conceal outcomes than it is to conceal corruption. Governments

---

1 Transparency International, 2013, "In Detail: Global Corruption Barometer 2013," www.transparency.org/gcb2013/in_detail.

and donors in particular should focus their measurement efforts on these outcome indicators. Ensuring that outcomes have been delivered will be a powerful tool to limit the extent of corruption and its impact on development.

What Are Expert Perception Measures Measuring?

Every year, with considerable fanfare, Transparency International launches the latest version of CPI,[2] which is perhaps the best known measure of a country's level of sleaze, closely followed by the Worldwide Governance Indicators (WGI) control of corruption measure. Because both sets of indicators use survey data on bribes and rankings provided by experts to create a mashed-up measure of overall corruption in a country, it should come as little surprise they correlate very closely with one another (see figure 2-1). But what exactly are the measures capturing: petty corruption, grand corruption, or something else?

The WGI team hopes that they are "capturing perceptions of the extent to which public power is exercised for private gain, including both petty and grand forms of corruption, as well as 'capture' of the state by elites and private interests."[3] And it is important to note that the indicators are measuring *something* with a fair level of accuracy. Perception measures of corruption appear reasonably stable over time, and they correlate with a number of expected objective indicators such as broad measures of development and factors such as the extent of regulation. Perceptions of corruption in a given country are also broadly correlated across different surveys, even when the survey collects responses from noticeably different groups. Nonetheless, there are reasons to believe that these broad indexes are not the best measures of either the corruption that firms and individuals care about or levels of grand corruption. If anything, these indexes are closest to measures of petty bribe payments.

The WGI use 31 sources of data to measure six dimensions of (perceptions of) governance from 1996 to 2014: (1) voice and accountability,

---

2 Transparency International, n.d., "Overview," www.transparency.org/research/cpi/over view.

3 Kaufmann, Kraay, and Mastruzzi (2010, p. 4).

Figure 2-1. Worldwide Governance Indicators' Control of Corruption
Is Highly Correlated with Transparency International's Corruption
Perceptions Index

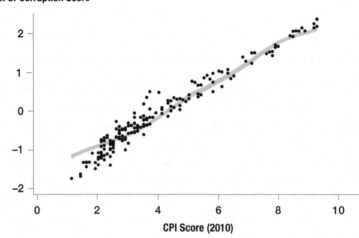

Sources: Transparency International CPI and WGI, 2010 data.

(2) political stability and absence of violence, (3) government effectiveness, (4) regulatory quality, (5) rule of law, and (6) control of corruption.[4]
The authors take individual data sources and assign them to six baskets,
one for each of the dimensions. They then produce a single measure from
each basket.[5]

The lead WGI researchers note that their classification of indicators
into particular categories (control of corruption versus government effectiveness, as it might be) is "not meant to be definitive. . . . Rather, it simply
reflects our views of what constitutes a consistent and useful organization
of the data."[6] As Laura Langbein and Stephen Knack from the World Bank

---

4 For more detailed information, see the World Bank's WGI information page at http://
info.worldbank.org/governance/wgi/index.aspx.

5 Using an unobserved components model described in detail in Kaufmann, Kraay, and
Mastruzzi (2010). The authors also publish (valuable) margins of error around their
scores to indicate the extent of variance between the data sources, but they do not capture any bias, reticence, error, or ignorance that is correlated across measures, nor do
they help establish what "the underlying measure" is actually measuring.

6 Kaufmann, Kraay, and Mastruzzi (2010, p. 11).

suggest, this admission raises concerns about "concept validity"—that indicators in one governance category are systematically related more to that category than to other categories.[7]

That concern is reflected in a very high correlation between the various WGI components. The indicators for control of corruption, rule of law, and government effectiveness are correlated with one another at 0.95, while the indicators for government effectiveness and regulatory quality indicators are correlated at 0.96, according to Melissa Thomas from Johns Hopkins.[8] A correlation of 1.00 is perfect, and these correlations are very close to that.

It would be fallacious to expect *government effectiveness* or *voice and accountability* to not overlap with a conception of *control of corruption*. But because these are complex and overlapping concepts being measured with some error, evaluators should be concerned that the indicators are not in fact able to significantly distinguish differences between the underlying realities related to each concept.[9] The statistical method being used may have uncovered an underlying reality of the control of corruption, but it is also possible that statistics may show an underlying reality of broad-based development, places that are better at hiding corruption, or something else entirely.

That makes *control of corruption* ontologically distinct from *child mortality* as an indicator, for example. Child mortality relates to a particular, distinct, and well-defined phenomenon (death) in a particular, distinct, and well-defined group (children under five years of age). Control of corruption is an undeliniated and unmeasured set of actions around a loosely defined concept. It is plausible to imagine measuring child mortality precisely, with no significant argument over the resulting statistic as a mea-

---

7 Langbein and Knack (2010).

8 Thomas (2009). Langbein and Knack (2010) perform factor analysis and conclude that all six WGI indicators correlate with the first factor with loadings over 75.

9 The authors of the WGI point out that very high correlation does not by itself demonstrate that the governance indicators are not measuring different phenomena. Education and earnings are very highly correlated, they note, but this does not mean education and earnings are not two separate things (Kaufmann, Kraay, and Mastruzzi [2010]). But the analogy is imperfect: education and earnings are two different things, each of which can be well measured. Evaluators cannot apply the same certainty to control of corruption and government effectiveness.

sure of what it seeks to describe. The same is completely untrue of control of corruption. The creators of the WGI are hopeful that the measure of control of corruption reflects reality in some meaningful sense, but that remains a hope.[10]

All that said, what is the empirical evidence linking the WGI corruption indicator with other measures? It is certainly related to the level of bribe payments across countries. For example, there is a significant relationship between the control of corruption measure and the percentage of citizens who report having paid a bribe (see figure 2-2). The World Bank Enterprise Surveys, conducted between 2005 and 2011, asked if firms regularly made payments to get things done and if firms in the industry were expected to pay bribes to secure a government contract. The correlation between the WGI control of corruption indicator in 2010 and those two questions are −0.69 and −0.63, respectively, meaning that a stronger control of corruption score is related to less bribe paying. There is also a significant although weaker relationship with bribes as a percentage of contract values (see figure 2-3).[11] The evidence above suggests that the control of corruption indicator has a closer relationship with petty bribery than with bribes for government contracts. This finding echoes the work of Stephen Knack from the World Bank, who demonstrated that Transparency International's corruption rankings correlate far more strongly with petty corruption in Eastern European survey data than with grand corruption as measured by bribe payments by firms to government officials.[12]

But (even) in terms of bribery, it is worth noting that previous analyses suggest that expert perception indicators do not add significantly to the predictive power of simple measures of GDP per capita when it comes to a relationship with petty bribery. Jakob Svensson from the Institute for International Economic Studies finds that cross-country survey evidence

---

10 See also Thomas (2009).

11 These correlations are Spearman's rank correlation coefficients.

12 Knack (2006). A comment from Transparency International staff on an earlier draft argued that the CPI is highly correlated with a measure of corruption extracted from data on antibribery cases brought under the OECD Convention (Escresa and Picci [2015]). The CPI and this measure are correlated at 0.78; however, the CPI and the Global Corruption Barometer data on petty bribe payments are correlated at 0.8, and all are highly correlated with GDP per capita.

regarding incidence of bribes is not significantly correlated with expert perceptions once GDP per capita is taken into account.[13]

Similar results hold at the firm level when using Transparency International's CPI, GDP per capita, and the World Bank Enterprise Survey data on the size of bribes required to secure government contracts.[14] The level of bribes paid in government contracting reported by firms at the national level is insignificantly related to the CPI once GDP per capita is controlled for. Surveyed corruption in contracting is significantly related to the percentage of managers who suggest that corruption is a serious issue in the same Enterprise Survey, and there is also a link between the percentage of managers listing corruption as a significant problem and CPI scores. But the correlation is weaker than that between survey results and GDP per capita. In short, the CPI is linked to measures of petty corruption, grand corruption as measured by reported bribes for contracts, and managers' perceptions of the state of the corruption issue, but it is not as closely linked as simple measures of GDP per capita.

Perhaps the CPI or the control of corruption measures are capturing some nonbribery elements of corruption better than survey evidence of bribe payments or domestic perceptions of the state of the corruption problem. It is difficult to answer this question empirically. That said, there are reasons to wonder if perception measures are capturing elements of corruption that are not (or cannot be) uncovered by surveys of bribe payments, rather than simply adding noise to the information contained in a bribe measure.

First, personal expectations and biases can create a big gap between perceptions and reality. In 2009, Ben Olken of Harvard University examined the relationship between people's perceptions of corruption in road building in villages in Indonesia and actual, audited levels of material theft from the projects.[15] He found that villagers' perceptions regarding corruption in a particular project in their own village was very weakly related to his objective measure of corruption. A 10 percent increase in the objective measure of corruption (an increase in missing expenditures equal to 2.4 percent of the total) is associated with a mere 0.3 percent increase

---

13 Svensson (2005).

14 Details of the survey are presented in Batra, Kaufmann, and Stone (2003).

15 Olken (2009).

Figure 2-2. Control of Corruption Is Correlated with Reports of Paying Bribes

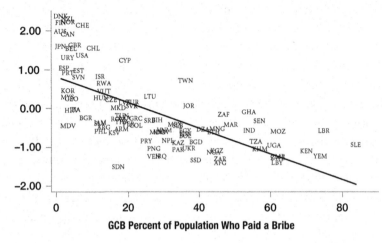

Sources: WGI and World Bank Enterprise Surveys.

Figure 2-3. Control of Corruption Is Moderately Correlated with Bribing for Contracts

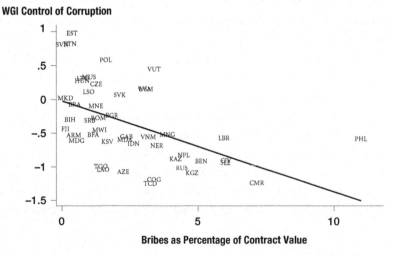

Sources: WGI and World Bank Enterprise Surveys.

in the probability that a respondent would perceive corruption. Indeed, perceived levels of corruption were driven far more by general cynicism about the honesty of politicians, the education level of respondents, and the ethnic diversity of the village than they were by measured levels of corruption. And while perceptions of corruption were considerably higher in ethnically diverse villages, objective evidence of corruption was considerably lower. In a 2014 assessment, Dilyan Donchev from the International Finance Corporation and Gergely Ujhelyi of the University of Houston have found that, across countries, the characteristics of respondents such as education, age, or employment status and the characteristics of firms such as the number of competitors, export experience, and recent layoffs all influence corruption perceptions from the Transparency International Global Corruption Barometer survey of individual bribe experience and perceptions of corruption from Enterprise Surveys.[16]

If such problems of bias plague perceptions of corruption in a particular project or country well known to survey respondents, imagine the issues with questionnaires asking for country-level perceptions from international respondents, many of whom may never have set foot in the economy being judged. In fact, "experts" appear unable to report with reliability even on the most visible forms of corruption. In 2006, Mireille Razafindrakoto and Francois Rouboud from the French Research Institute for Development compared perceptions of corruption from a (nonrandom) survey of 329 officials, aid workers, and other self-selected experts in corruption in Africa to survey responses from within countries for eight sub-Saharan countries. An average of 13 percent of the populations across the eight countries said that they had been direct victims of corruption over the past year. This survey response compared to an expert estimate of 52 percent. In every country, surveyed levels of corruption were dramatically different from expert estimation. But the ratio of expert estimate of victimization compared to surveyed report of victimization varied considerably by country (see table 2-1).[17]

Note that this is not a case of asking a different question or of interpretation—experts were not thinking about grand corruption or impact while survey respondents were thinking about petty corruption or

---

16 Donchev and Ujhelyi (2014). See also Roca (2011), Kaplan and Pathania (2010), and TNS Opinion & Social (2014).

17 Razafindrakoto and Roubaud (2010)

bribe size. When asked to estimate the survey response, the experts failed, badly and inconsistently. For example, experts imagine Burkina Faso to be comparatively free of corruption; survey estimates suggest the opposite. If experts do this poorly in estimating the most easily observed forms of corruption, there is considerable risk in assuming they are better at estimating levels of overall "system-stacked" corruption.

A second reason to doubt the special insight of expert perceptions regarding grand corruption is that they fail to indicate when massive corruption really is happening at the highest levels. Take the case of Peru's CPI score. In 2000, tapes of the head of Peru's National Intelligence Service, Vladimiro Montesinos, bribing legislators, judges, television station operators, and others—a total of 1,600 people—led to Montesinos' ouster and President Alberto Fujimori's impeachment. They also precipitated a significant deterioration in the country's CPI score. But the collapse in the CPI came *after* the tapes were released. There was no significant change in the index before the release of the tapes, when Peru was perceived as being cleaner than the Czech Republic, for example. Of course, the actual corruption was going on before the tapes were released.[18]

A similar example of perception failure is that of Brazil. In 2013, Brazilian authorities uncovered a scandal involving state-owned oil company Petrobras, which involved $5.3 billion in payments to workers and politicians over a decade. The country's current president was chair of the Petrobras board over that time, the country's house speaker had been indicted on related charges, and by 2016 more than half of both houses of Brazil's congress were facing charges of corruption or other serious crimes.[19] In 2003, around when the Petrobras corruption began, Brazil had a score of 39 out of 100 on Transparency International's CPI. (A score of 100 suggests that a country is angelically free of corruption.) That score compared to Italy's 2003 score of 53. By 2010, the two countries were statistically neck-and-neck on the perceptions score; in 2012, Brazil briefly overtook Italy in terms of being comparatively more free of perceived corruption. Only in 2015 did Brazil's CPI ranking fall notably below Italy's level and below its 2003 score. Once again, the CPI lagged the scandal.[20]

---

18 Ausland and Tolmos (2005).
19 Beauchamp (2016).
20 Transparency International, "Overview."

Table 2-1. Experts Are Terrible at Predicting the Percentage of People Victimized by Corruption

	Expert estimate of percent of population who have been victims of corruption	Percent of population who say they have been a victim of corruption	Ratio
Benin	53.7	8.7	6.2
Burkina Faso	38.0	15.2	2.5
Côte d'Ivoire	58.2	16.5	3.5
Madagascar	54.0	16.3	3.3
Mali	49.1	10.1	4.9
Niger	53.4	8.2	6.5
Senegal	50.8	10.8	4.7
Togo	59.2	9.6	6.2

Source: Modified from Razafindrakoto and Roubaud (2006).

The index can also produce rather odd rankings depending on the nature of corruption. Indonesia, for instance, is ranked as considerably more corrupt than Saudi Arabia. To be fair, President Suharto of Indonesia was widely considered to be the world-leading premier in terms of corruption in his 31-year rule. Upper-end estimates suggest that his family amassed a $35 billion fortune—about 16 percent of Indonesia's market-rate GDP in 1997—during his time in office. But in 1996 the U.S. State Department estimated that just three members of Saudi Arabia's royal family had a combined fortune of $33 billion[21]—21 percent of Saudi Arabia's 1996 market-rate GDP.[22] Five or six princes controlled the revenues from one million barrels a day of Saudi Arabia's eight-million-barrel production at the time, family members made money by confiscating lands near the locations of upcoming investment projects or selling visas to expatriate workers, and annual government stipends to members of the family were worth $2 billion. As an example of the use of public office for private gain, it is hard to beat government payouts made simply on the grounds of being

---

21 Fowler (1996).

22 Data on GDP from World Bank World Development Indicators in current dollars are available at http://data.worldbank.org/data-catalog/world-development-indicators, accessed 1/21/2016.

a member of the royal family. Yet in 2003, the earliest year Transparency International ranked corruption levels in Saudi Arabia, the kingdom was ranked 46 out of 133; Indonesia was 122.[23] Apparently, according to the experts polled, the abuse of public office for private gain is not so bad if you wear a crown while doing it. But when it comes to impact on development, it may be as bad or worse.

A third reason to doubt that any one country-level indicator is meaningful applies not just to the CPI or the WGI but to any single measure of corruption at the national level. Given the many different types of corruption, and strong evidence that relative levels vary considerably by sector, process, and institutions within countries, no one indicator of control of corruption is likely to accurately reflect the full extent of corruption in a country. (The next section will discuss this issue at greater length.)

To summarize, measures like the CPI and the control of corruption measure, which are based largely on expert perceptions, do not correlate particularly well with the types of corruption that are comparatively easy to measure, such as bribes. Furthermore, there are good reasons to believe that they do a poor job of capturing the kinds of corruption that are harder to measure, like "systemic corruption." This problem is exacerbated by the fact that any one country-level indicator has to capture what is clearly a heterogeneous problem within countries across sectors and regions.

Can We Measure Bribes, At Least?

Indicators of bribe payments have an advantage over perception indicators of corruption: they are trying to measure a considerably less abstract concept. It is not always clear what is a bribe and what is a gift freely given without expectation of favor, but it is much more straightforward to measure bribe paying than to rate a country's control of corruption on a scale of one to ten. That said, measuring bribery still produces unreliable estimates.

One of the questions in the World Bank Enterprise Survey asks how large the "informal payments" needed to win a government contract are. In 22 countries the average is more than 5 percent of the value of the con-

---

23 Transparency International, 2003, "Corruption Perceptions Index 2003," www.trans parency.org/research/cpi/cpi_2003/0/.

tract. In 38 countries the average is between 2 and 5 percent; in 52 countries the average is below 2 percent. Corruption therefore acts as a real tax in many countries, not just on aid but on all government transactions. But these numbers are still open to some doubt.

J. Vernon Henderson from Brown University and Ari Kuncoro from the University of Indonesia suggest that differences in survey design and technique account for the gap between their estimates of corrupt payments of 10.5 percent of costs and the 3 percent found by the Indonesian Annual Survey of Medium and Large Enterprises.[24] Again, firm-level surveys in Africa suggest that the scale of reported petty corruption varies considerably, depending on how the question is posed. Firms in Africa that report the amount of bribes they pay as a percentage of sales suggest about 2.5 to 4.5 percent of sales go to petty bribes. Firms that report an absolute amount of bribe payments suggest amounts that are one-quarter to one-fifteenth of that percentage-based amount.

Or look at the Business Environment and Enterprise Performance Survey (BEEPS) of Eastern Europe, the largest and most detailed cross-country survey of petty and grand corruption that has been carried out. It covers more than 4,000 firms in 22 transition countries.[25] In 2008, out of 12,676 firms that report on frequency of bribing and bribes as a percentage of sales, 22 percent report that the bribes as a percentage of sales were zero, but also report that they sometimes pay bribes. Two percent report that bribes as a percentage of sales for firms like theirs were above zero despite the fact that firms like theirs never pay bribes. These responses suggest at least some inconsistency in reporting (see table 2-2).[26]

Additional uncertainty comes from reticence to report bad behavior and the element of perception involved when the question involves "firms like yours" rather than "your firm." Aart Kraay from the World Bank and Peter Murrell from the University of Maryland argue that there may be widespread *under*reporting of bribe payments, but that the level of reticence to report varies across countries, suggesting nonrandom error in

---

24 Henderson and Kuncoro (2006).

25 The World Bank, n.d., "Business Environment and Enterprise Performance Survey," http://data.worldbank.org/data-catalog/BEEPS. Details of the survey can be found in Hellman and others (2000).

26 Out of 12,676 firms that report an answer to question 39 (frequency of bribes) and 40 (bribes as percentage of sales).

Table 2-2. Firms Are Inconsistent in Their Reports of Bribe Paying

Reported bribes as a percentage of sales	Frequency of bribes	
	"Never" (%)	"Not never" (%)
0	35.4	22.3
>0	1.7	40.5

Source: World Bank, "Business Environment and Enterprise Performance Survey," 2008.

country-level corruption measures that rely on survey evidence. But it is also possible that bribe payments are being *over*estimated, as people assume that firms like theirs are more corrupt than their own firm.[27]

The scale of bribe payments in some cases that have been prosecuted suggests that bribes as a percentage of contract size are lower than surveys would suggest. Bribes involving contracts for the Lesotho Highlands dam amounted to about $6 million while project costs were $2.5 billion. Enron spent $20 million on "education and project development process" expenditures in the corrupt Dabhol power deal in India, a project that cost $1.3 billion.[28] Siemens paid $1.7 million in bribes related to 42 contracts under the Iraq oil-for-food program worth $80 million, $31 million in corrupt payments related to a $1 billion Argentinian national identity card project, and $19 million on bribes related to the Venezuelan Maracaibo and Velencia metro projects with combined costs of around $340 million, and a total of $5.3 million in corrupt payments related to a Bangladesh telecoms contract worth $41 million.[29] These figures are not from average deals—these are deals known to be particularly corrupt—yet the bribe payments as a percentage of contract values average 4.1 percent in these cases. And bribes as a percentage of total payments were larger on smaller contracts: only 1.6 percent of the total $5.2 billion value of these contracts was paid in bribes.[30]

Either way, survey questions are not exact, and they are open to subjec-

---

27 Kraay and Murrell (2016).

28 Kenny (2007, p. 5).

29 U.S. Department of Justice (2008).

30 Note that the OECD Foreign Bribery Report suggests an average payment of 11 percent of the transaction value across 427 cases of enforcement actions under the OECD bribery convention between 1999 and 2014.

tive interpretation. One cannot expect one person in a company to have perfect knowledge of company revenues, contract sizes, and, in particular, the size of bribes paid in "firms like theirs." Take, for example, one BEEPS question: "When firms in your industry do business with the government, how much of the contract value would they typically offer in additional or unofficial payments to secure the contract?" Using construction firms as an example, we can see how much BEEPS answers reveal about sector-level corruption. If construction firms were perfectly informed about the typical level of corrupt payments to government in their industry in their country, and they understood and answered the question in the same way, all firms would give similar answers. If corruption was stable over time, as suggested by slow-moving indicators like the CPI and control of corruption measures, those answers would be similar over time.

The results show otherwise. The sample size of construction firms in each country is small, which adds noise, but nonetheless the results suggest that the idea of a stable, constant, and well-known schedule of fees for bribes affecting firms appears not to apply. For 2005 data, the average answer across countries is 1.48 percent of sales to bribes. The average of the standard deviations is 2.33 percent. Clearly, all firms in the same industry in the same country do not give the same answer (see table 2-3). When reviewing the answers for bribes as a percentage of sales in 2002 and 2005, the average levels and variance in answers appear to have changed dramatically over that period. In just over three years, average bribe payments apparently fell by 28 percent as a proportion of sales across these countries. And the relationship between average levels over time is weak: Tajikistan, for example, was 18th out of 27 in terms of the ascending value of bribe payments in 2002 but reported the smallest bribe payments in 2005.

There are many different types of firms, and they frequently will be working with different levels of government or different departments within those levels. And levels of corruption can surely change over three years. But if these factors account for the variability of responses, it suggests the danger of assuming that one indicator can accurately gauge levels of corruption even for one distinct sector-level activity at one time, let alone all activities nationwide and over time.

Table 2-3. Construction Firms Do Not Agree about Bribes as a Percentage of Sales in Construction

	2002		2005	
	Mean (%)	Stdev	Mean (%)	Stdev[a]
Turkey	0.04	0.18	1.70	2.00
Estonia	0.31	0.54	0.68	1.70
Armenia	0.36	0.90	2.20	3.90
Macedonia	0.57	0.70	1.70	2.30
Bosnia-Herzegovina	0.65	1.10	0.43	0.82
Slovenia	0.89	4.30	0.43	1.30
Croatia	1.10	2.40	1.30	3.00
Lithuania	1.10	2.60	1.10	1.70
Hungary	1.30	2.10	1.60	2.80
Uzbekistan	1.50	3.40	2.60	4.00
Belarus	1.60	2.80	2.00	3.40
Poland	1.70	2.80	1.30	2.40
Slovakia	1.70	2.60	2.60	4.00
Yugoslavia	1.70	3.00	1.10	2.60
Latvia	1.80	2.90	0.92	1.40
Czech Rep	1.90	2.60	1.20	2.00
Bulgaria	2.10	3.30	1.30	2.40
Moldova	2.20	4.10	0.50	0.84
Russia	2.30	3.10	1.40	1.70
Kazakhstan	2.70	4.70	1.80	3.30
Georgia	2.80	1.80	0.50	1.00
Ukraine	3.20	4.20	0.50	0.89
Tajikistan	3.80	4.90	0.10	0.39
Romania	4.00	4.50	0.90	1.60
Azerbaijan	4.20	5.50	3.70	5.10
Kyrgyz Rep	4.30	5.40	4.10	4.30
Albania	6.20	4.60	2.40	2.20
Ireland	-	-	0.28	1.50
Serbia	-	-	1.20	1.70

Source: World Bank, "Business Environment and Enterprise Performance Survey."

a. Stdev = standard deviation of the variable.

Can Any One Measure of Corruption Reflect a Complex Underlying Reality?

In that regard, it is worth noting that the relative levels of surveyed bribe payments vary considerably within countries. Table 2-4 shows the country-level correlations of different bribe and gift indicators from the World Bank Enterprise Surveys. The correlations between different corruption measures are strongly significant, but still vary from 0.40 to 0.83.

Figure 2-4 lists countries by income and reports on the country average and standard deviation of answers to the eight questions on the expectation of gifts. It is clear that the average firm in some countries reports more corruption than the average firm in others, and that higher incomes are associated with lower bribe payments, but there is often significant variation within countries between the indicators, reflecting different levels of bribery across government functions. Similarly, there is no significant correlation between cross-industry estimates of bribe payments and estimates of bribe payments given by the subset of construction industries at the national level in a sample of eastern European and Central Asian countries covered by BEEPS.[31] Any statement about a country being more bribe-prone than another would need to specify the type of bribery to provide an accurate reflection of the situation.

The Harm of Bribery Varies

Added to measurement issues is the gap between such measures and the damage actually done by corruption. Corruption that raises costs but still delivers good-quality goods and services, for instance, is less of a problem than corruption that interferes with the delivery of those goods and services. Imagine a road project that costs $1 million to build but generates $300,000 in economic returns each year for 10 years after construction. The project's overall economic rate of return is about 30 percent (the average return for World Bank transport projects completed in the recent past). If collusive bidding had raised the project's price of construction by

---

31 Kenny (2006).

Table 2-4. The Correlation between Enterprise Surveys Corruption Indicators Is Strong, but Not Perfect

Percentage of firms expected to give gifts . . .	to public officials (to "get things done")	in meetings with tax officials	to secure a government contract	to get an operating license	to get an import license	to get a construction permit	to get an electrical connection
in meetings with tax officials	0.828						
to secure a government contract	0.707	0.663					
to get an operating license	0.701	0.799	0.567				
to get an import license	0.606	0.645	0.400	0.669			
to get a construction permit	0.669	0.700	0.577	0.725	0.669		
to get an electrical connection	0.677	0.694	0.507	0.642	0.554	0.641	
to get a water connection	0.553	0.610	0.404	0.592	0.580	0.614	0.741

Source: Authors' calculations using World Bank Enterprise Survey data, available from www.enterprisesurveys.org/.

Figure 2-4. Survey Responses on Bribery Have Wide Variance within Countries

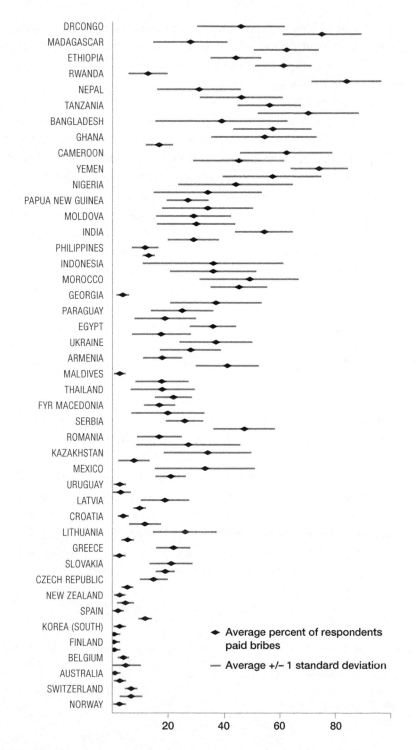

20 percent, to $1.2 million, its rate of return would drop to 26 percent.[32] This is a significant decline, but it still leaves the project at more than double the World Bank's traditional "hurdle rate" of 10 percent return necessary to justify the investment.

Imagine instead that the bidder agreed to a contract price of $1 million, but used insufficient and substandard materials to build the road, spending only $800,000 on construction and pocketing the remaining $200,000. This type of corruption reduces the road's traffic capacity so that yearly economic returns fall by one-quarter, and shortens the useful life of the road to five years. The overall rate of return would be only 15 percent.[33] Compared with the collusive bidding example above, the same financial level of corruption has a considerably larger economic impact in this case, reducing the rate of return by 15 percent rather than 4 percent.

What if construction firms then used $200,000 to pay off legislators to divert money from operations and maintenance funds for the construction of the road and recouped their expenditure through overbidding or poor construction? At this point, with the new road project sucking up resources from maintenance of existing roads, reducing traffic capacities and road life across the network, economic rates of return might turn negative.

Again, some acts of petty bribery are worse than others. To some degree, petty bribes in the water sector, for instance, are payments for services that undercompensated employees should be providing anyway. They are a transfer to get the job done, perhaps one of the least harmful forms of corruption. Compared to payments that encourage illegal activities, or payments to avoid law enforcement, payments to encourage legal activities have less impact on economic outcomes. And corruption that reduces the quality of water services and diverts connections is likely to be a far larger source of economic harm than the financial scale of petty bribes for connections.

Looking more broadly, levels of corruption in water provision in South

---

32 This (and subsequent calculations) view the corrupt payment as a transfer but accounts for a (high) marginal cost of government funds lost to corruption of 1.50 (a 50 percent deadweight loss). See Kenny (2006) for details.

33 This is approximately the economic impact of poor road construction suggested by Olken (2007).

Asia in 2001–02 provide evidence of this impact above bribery.[34] Contractors frequently paid bribes to win contracts worth between 1 and 6 percent of contract values, followed by kickbacks during construction of between 6 and 11 percent of the contract value, and formed "sanctioned" cartels that raised prices by 15 to 20 percent. Kickbacks also went to cover low-quality work, in which materials worth between 3 and 5 percent of the contract value are not supplied. Assuming an economic impact of each dollar of such missing materials of between $3 and $4 in terms of shorter life and limited capacity, this suggests an economic cost equal to 9–20 percent of already-inflated contract prices. These two forms of corruption together may have raised the price of a sustainable water connection by 25 to 45 percent. Compared to total petty and grand corrupt financial payments per water connection of between $29 and $69, the economic damage of this corruption was closer to $101–$181.[35]

Even this calculation only partially accounts for the potential impact of corruption. Some of the most damaging results involve the construction of infrastructure that carries almost no economic value at all. Returning to the case of Enron in Maharashtra, the level of bribery may have approached $20 million, but the economic cost of the corruption approached $1.3 billion because the plant was never economical to run.[36] Or look at the benefit of bribery to firms. Based on 166 bribery cases involving publicly listed firms between 1971 and 2007, Yan Leung Cheung from Hong Kong Baptist University and colleagues estimate that each dollar a firm paid in bribes raised its stock price by $11, suggesting the considerable majority of the rents being transferred through corruption go to the firm doing the bribing rather than to the officials taking the bribes (although high-ranking officials do better at appropriating rents).[37]

Even if evaluators had good measures of the bribery involving firms, they would provide a very poor measure of development impact. Yet there is no evidence that general perceptions of the control of corruption are

---

34 Davis (2004).

35 This uses an assumption of a $400 cost of connection from Fay and Yepes (2003) and a $3–4 cost per dollar of missing materials based on an estimate for road construction from Olken (2007), which clearly needs to be treated with caution when applied to a completely different infrastructure sector.

36 Gulati and Rao (2006).

37 Cheung, Rau, and Stouraitis (2012).

any better at capturing these economic costs. The fact that these perceptions have a weak link with economic *outcomes* (as we will see in the next chapter) suggests that they do an imperfect job of showing the true scope of the problem.

In short, the nature of corruption can have a significant impact on the economic damage caused by that corruption, even if the financial losses are the same size. Bribery payments made to deliver high-quality projects and services at inflated prices may be far less damaging than corrupt activities that impact the quality of delivery or the type of projects undertaken. But there are no good indicators of "corruption impact," if that term indicates the impact of corruption on the actual delivery of adequate-quality goods and services to intended recipients.

What Do Normal People Mean by Corruption?

A recent Transparency International survey in Papua New Guinea asked respondents to define corruption. About one-third of respondents suggested a definition along the lines of *abuse of public office for private gain*—a common technical definition itself far broader than bribery—but the majority provided other answers. Its meaning can change from person to person, suggests the Transparency International report:

> An older woman in East New Britain may complain bitterly about the "corruption" occurring in her village with unmarried people engaging in sexual relations. A young Engan man may feel angry about the "corruption" occurring when his MP fails to pay for funerals or school fees. A middle-aged public servant in Port Moresby despairs about "corruption" when his colleagues demand a cash payment before processing contractor invoices.[38]

---

38 Walton and Dix (2013). Note also what is considered morally unacceptable behavior from an official can be highly context specific. Søreide, Tostensen, and Skage (2012) find that managers offer whole departments a few days of per diem travel compensation simply as a general reward, with no expectation of travel. Perhaps this is in an effort to win loyalty or reduce the wage gap with the private sector; regardless, those involved do not perceive this practice as corrupt.

This phenomenon is hardly unique to Papua New Guinea. Depending on context, a so-called speed payment for an electricity connection or a license might be thought of as bribe or simply a tip for service. Taking a stopover on a government-paid flight to visit relatives might be a perk or embezzlement. Helping a niece get an interview for a job in a friend's department could be nepotism or just being a good uncle. And there is disagreement over the need for corruption to involve someone in a government position—private firms, nongovernmental organizations, and the media are all seen as corrupt by many poll respondents, a fair enough position given the dictionary definition of the term.

The issue of what constitutes corruption was part of the recent U.S. Supreme Court ruling that considerably loosened the constraints on campaign-finance limits.[39] Between ruling and dissent, one of the things that the justices argued over was the nature of corruption, or at least the corruption that they should have been worried about. The majority opinion suggested that the only corruption that mattered was the quid pro quo variety (payments for favors), while dissenters favored a broader concern—the general corrupting influence of money in the system. The debate was a good illustration of the problem that researchers face when they try to put a number on the level of corruption.

Quid pro quo corruption is what surveyors are trying to measure when they ask questions about informal payments. Pay a government official a bribe, and in return they will provide you with a service, or a contract, or a place in the school or clinic (or not arrest you, or not deny you something you are entitled to). But when researchers ask people how corrupt they think the government is, respondents do not just think about bribe payments. They think about all sorts of different ways government officials use public office for private gain, many of which do not involve direct payoffs and some of which may not be illegal. Think of U.S. Congress members using inside information they gain from their jobs to try (successfully or unsuccessfully) to make money in the stock market.[40] Or bureaucrats stealing office supplies and skipping work. Or politicians steering projects and government contracts to friends in their home districts with hope

---

39 *McCutcheon et al. v. Federal Election Commission* 572 U. S. slip op. (2013), available at www.supremecourt.gov/opinions/13pdf/12-536_e1pf.pdf.

40 Eggers and Hainmueller (2013).

of future favor (such as votes, political contributions, or jobs after retirement) but no explicit deal for a payoff.

These differing concepts of corruption are one reason why there is often a considerable gap between surveyed corruption as measured in a quid pro quo, bribe-paying sense and surveyed corruption measured in a broader perceptions sense. Take, for instance, the institution over which the Supreme Court presides—the U.S. judiciary. In surveys that ask Americans about corruption in the U.S. courts system, 42 percent of respondents view the judiciary as corrupt or extremely corrupt, while 15 percent of those who had contact with the courts reported paying a bribe to a member of the judiciary over the past 12 months.[41] When you ask citizens themselves if corruption in general is prevalent in their country, they are thinking about a lot more than bribe payments. They are more concerned about whether the government and the political system are fair or stacked against them.

Note this broader idea of corruption is what the WGI control of corruption measure is supposedly trying to reflect: public power for private gain and elite capture. Yet it appears to be a better measure of bribe payments. And using the stacked-system concept of corruption as perceived by *citizens* rather than *experts* there are good reasons to think that the difference between the United States and developing countries is not all that large. Corruption is seen as a significant problem even in many of the world's richest nations where bribes are very rare (see figure 2-5).

Figure 2-6 relates the proportion of people in a country who reported having paid a bribe in the past 12 months with the average answer to "To what extent do you think that corruption is a problem in the public sector in this country?" on a scale of one to five. Respondents in Denmark, Finland, Rwanda, and Sudan, for example, all suggest that corruption is a minor problem and few report paying bribes, while respondents in Kenya, Sierra Leone, and Liberia report high concern and high levels of bribe payment. Experience paying a bribe is by far the most significant correlate with perceptions of corruption at the individual level,[42] but nonetheless the relationship is far from perfect. Respondents in Portugal, Spain, and Italy sug-

---

41　Transparency International, 2013, "United States," www.transparency.org/gcb2013/country?country=united_states.

42　Birdsall, Diofasi, and Kenny (forthcoming).

Figure 2-5. Corruption Is Perceived as a Big Problem Even in Countries Where Bribes Are Rare

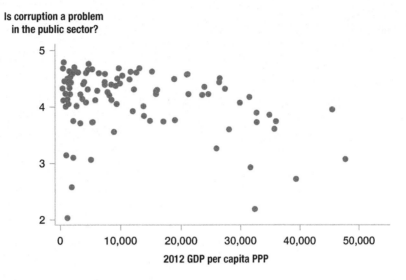

Sources: Transparency International Global Corruption Barometer; and World Bank World Development Indicators.

gest that corruption is a bigger problem than do respondents from Kenya or Sierra Leone, even though fewer than 5 percent of the European respondents have paid a bribe.[43] (Cross-country comparability of perceptions questions should be regarded with caution: people from some countries or cultures might think of a two on a scale of one to five the same as others view a three. This measure is likely to be particularly noisy.)

When people around the world are asked if corruption is a problem in particular institutions in their country, the relationship between economic development and their answers can become even weaker. People in poor countries are more likely than respondents in rich countries to say that the police and the judiciary are corrupt. Fewer than one-third of people in the United Kingdom and about two-fifths in the United States think that the police are corrupt; it is 82 percent in Pakistan and 92 per-

---

43 See Abramo (2008) for further investigation of this relationship.

Figure 2-6. The Weak Link between Bribe Payments and Views of Corruption as a Problem

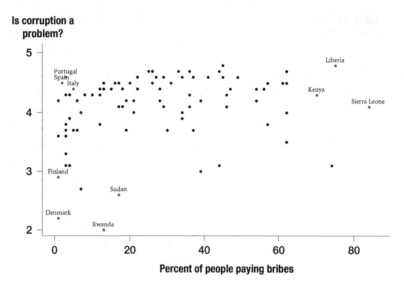

Source: Transparency International Global Corruption Barometer, 2013.

cent in Ghana. But there is pretty much no relationship between views of business corruption and GDP per capita. And when it comes to the media and political parties, people in richer countries are actually slightly more likely to say these institutions are corrupt or very corrupt than are citizens of poorer countries. In the United States, 76 percent of the public thinks political parties are corrupt, the same proportion as in Romania, Ghana, Pakistan, and the Democratic Republic of the Congo (see figure 2-7).

Again, looking at business surveys, the corruption that appears to concern firms the most is not well reflected in levels of bribe payments. The link between the proportion of firms that suggest that corruption is a major constraint at the country level and the percentage of firms that are expected to give gifts or average bribes as a percentage of sales is very weak. Many countries with a very low proportion of firms reporting that they are expected to bribe for government favor nonetheless have more than 50 percent of firms reporting that corruption is a major constraint to business (see figure 2-8).

A respondent's answer to questions about the corruption of political parties or legislatures is more closely related to how he or she answers the question "To what extent is this country's government run by a few big entities acting in their own best interests?" than it is to reported bribe payments. This finding suggests that respondents consider political corruption to have more to do with elites using the power of government to their own advantage than with the more narrow issue of bureaucrats asking for money.[44]

They may have a point: not least, there is evidence that (legal) lobbying is far more effective than outright bribery at steering favors and legislation.[45] In Brazil, firms that specialize in public works projects and donate to a ruling-party candidate who then wins an election can expect an increase in government contracts worth 21 times the value of their contributions.[46] This is not a problem limited to developing countries: between 1994 and 2009, when Silvio Berlusconi was prime minister of Italy three times, his television station Mediaset received an estimated €1 billion of additional advertising revenue largely from companies operating in highly regulated sectors. Stefano DellaVigna from the University of California–Berkeley and colleagues estimate a similar magnitude in returns to those companies from regulatory change over the same period.[47]

The financial returns of holding office also do not appear to be dramatically different across democracies rich and poor. Raymond Fisman from Boston University and his colleagues, for example, have found that the annual asset growth of Indian parliamentarians over an election cycle is three to six percentage points higher than for runners-up, mostly accounted for by 13–20 percentage point higher asset returns among the Council of Ministers.[48] This is a large discrepancy, but given average assets of about $200,000 at the election, it only amounts to about a $300,000 excess asset gain for each of the very few most powerful politicians in India

---

44 See also Abramo (2008) on the strong relationship between perceptions of corruption from the Global Corruption Barometer and opinions about broader issues such as human rights.

45 Campos and Giovannoni (2007).

46 Boas, Hidalgo, and Richardson (2014). Given the risk of the candidate losing and margins on contracting work, this return may not be as spectacular as it sounds.

47 DellaVigna and others (2013).

48 Fisman, Schulz, and Vig (2012).

Figure 2-7. Perceived Corruption Is Not Always Lower in Rich Countries

Police Corrupt

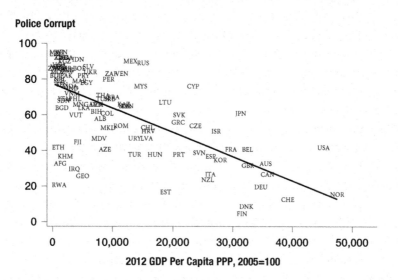

2012 GDP Per Capita PPP, 2005=100

Judiciary Corrupt

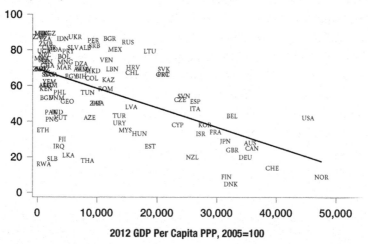

2012 GDP Per Capita PPP, 2005=100

Public Officials / Civil Servants Corrupt

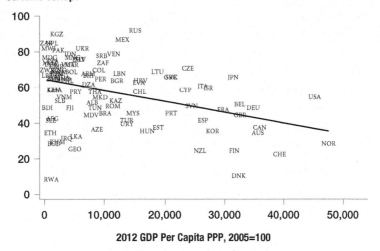

2012 GDP Per Capita PPP, 2005=100

Political Parties Corrupt

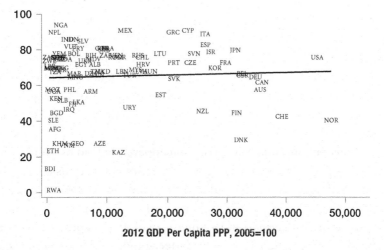

2012 GDP Per Capita PPP, 2005=100

Sources: Transparency International Global Corruption Barometer and World Bank World Development Indicators.

Figure 2-8. The Weak Link between Firm Bribe Payments and Concern with Corruption

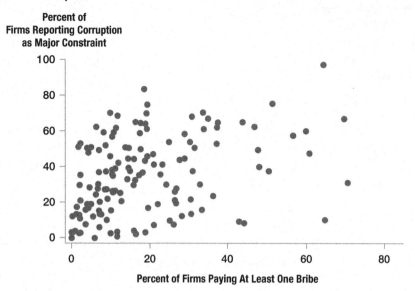

Source: World Bank Enterprise Surveys.

over five years. The results are not too different from a study of the returns of serving in the British Parliament, where conservative members of Parliament (MPs) who narrowly won an election ended up twice as rich as those who narrowly lost, largely thanks to outside employment possibilities while they were MPs.[49] There is nothing illegal in this outcome and no legally defined bribes are paid, but there is certainly a private payoff to public service.

The broader conception of corruption apparently held by poll respondents is closely linked to concern with extractive institutions designed to favor a small elite, as highlighted by scholars of institutions and development such as Daron Acemoglu, Simon Johnson, and James Robinson alongside Stanley Engerman and Kenneth Sokoloff. (Chapter 3 will review their work on this topic.) To take the latter authors, their concern is over "institutional structures that greatly advantaged members of elite classes

---

49 Eggers and Hainmueller (2009).

(and disadvantaging the bulk of the population) by providing them with more political influence and access to economic opportunities."[50]

Europe and the United States have created tax systems, corporate subsidies, intellectual-property rules, safety nets for financial institutions, and regulations on trade, land use, and school systems that help insulate the rich from competition from the poor and ensure that considerable inequality persists.[51] Developing countries have done the same. In some cases bribe payments are an additional tool, but they add little to the cumulative effect: inequality is no higher on average in poor countries than in rich ones, which might suggest that neither is the impact of policies and institutions a factor in driving inequality. The top 10 percent of households in the United States shared 44 percent of total post-tax income in 2004 (the figure is higher today).[52] In the United Kingdom, the top decile shares 34 percent of total household income.[53] The average for the 78 developing countries with data from the World Bank over the past five years is a top income share of 32 percent. At the least, if poor countries are more corrupt than rich countries, the elite in those countries must be remarkably less effective at using corruption to concentrate wealth.[54]

Again, this is not to say corruption is not a problem, nor that particular forms are not more common in developing countries. It is to suggest that the kind of policies and practices that skew outcomes in favor of the elite appear to be about as common in many rich countries as in many poor countries. This may be closer to the kind of corruption likely to be behind poor economic performance than bribe payments.[55] (Chapter 3 will discuss evidence for this perspective in greater detail.) It also may be closer to the kind of corruption that appears to drive popular perceptions. But if this is the sort of corruption that matters, it is not the sort of corruption captured by the expert perception measures used by aid agencies.

---

50 Engerman and Sokoloff (2002, abstract).

51 See Milanovic (2016).

52 Piketty and Saez (2006).

53 Resolution Foundation, February 11, 2014, "The State of Living Standards," www.resolutionfoundation.org/publications/state-living-standards/.

54 Thanks to Bill Savedoff for that observation in his review comments on this book.

55 Ostry and Berg (2011); Ostry, Berg, and Tsangarides (2014); and Cingano (2014). But see also Kraay (2015).

Conclusion—Measuring What Really Matters

There is a considerable literature on our inability to accurately perceive the scale of risks that are complex, ill understood, and frequent topics in the media—for example, nuclear power and terrorism.[56] Corruption apparently falls into the same category. Broadly, everyone everywhere thinks that everyone else is on the take. British people, for example, think that about one-quarter of all benefits payments are fraudulently claimed, while the best estimate is closer to 1 percent.[57] Surveys run by the European Union suggest that three-quarters of respondents think corruption is widespread in their own country, and a similar proportion think that bribery is the easiest way to get some public services. But while one-quarter of respondents say they think it is acceptable to do a favor or give a gift to get a public service, only 1 in 20 say that they have actually done so. Perhaps this finding suggests that there is a problem on the demand side. Perhaps the public (and expert) perception is wrong. Perhaps public servants are not always as corrupt as people think.[58]

Or to take an example from Indonesia, where there is a widespread sense that decentralization has increased the country's corruption problem. Vivi Alatas from the World Bank and colleagues found that local elites and their families on average were no more likely than would be expected to receive targeted government welfare payments, and although those in formal leadership positions did see a slight advantage, eliminating elite capture entirely would improve the welfare gains from the programs by less than 1 percent. This outcome is true despite the fact that elites are legally empowered with considerable influence over the allocation of those programs. Weak administrative data were a far greater culprit than corruption in the project's poor targeting and impact.[59]

Either a widespread culture of corruption across the world is an overplayed idea, or the corruption is taking place through legal channels or is otherwise uncaptured by measures of diversion or bribe payment. Corruption in the broad, popular sense of the term may well be more rampant than suggested by bribe surveys or the CPI—especially in rich countries.

---

56 Siegel (2005).
57 Paige (2013).
58 TNS Opinion & Social (2014).
59 Alatas and others (2013).

But the problem remains that corruption indicators are not well designed to reflect this broader abuse.

It appears that expert corruption perceptions measure neither the corruption that nationals most care about nor (we will see) the corruption that most matters to development. While firm and individual surveys give a far more accurate picture of bribery, it appears they do best at measuring the petty corruption that (once again) is not necessarily a major barrier to development as reflected in popular opinion or economic analysis. The weakness of existing corruption measures may help to explain why the evidence base for anticorruption interventions is so limited, as the subsequent chapters will indicate.

There is an alternative for countries or donors wanting to judge the quality of governance or the impact of malfeasance. It is to measure outputs and outcomes, including those outcomes that can be derailed by weak institutions and corruption. We can measure some corruption as part of the quality of service delivery (such as inappropriate payments or absenteeism), along with outputs related to corruption (such as road quality or electricity transmission and distribution losses) or indicators covering outcomes (such as the proportion of people passing a driving test who can actually drive). Such measures are easier to compile with accuracy and are likely to be far better indicators of any reduction in the development impact—the results delivered—of corruption.

It is time to change the current approach to focus on measuring what matters. And looking at what matters, it becomes apparent that the current measures of corruption are inadequate and at best distantly related to the outcomes we care about. The next chapter focuses on this link between corruption measures and development outcomes.

3

Development Predestinationism

Trade and the free market, industrial policy or Internet connectivity—there is a long list of potential cures suggested as silver bullets for the condition of poverty. Weak governance and corruption is the latest lead bullet—a malady of maladies following on from poor policies (for which the cure was structural adjustment), poor well-being (human-centered development), and poor capitalists (filling the finance gap). It is also the most leaden of all—the development community knows to move capital, knows how to improve health and (to some extent) education, and even has a pretty good idea about how to reduce inflation. But improving weak governance is apparently a historically laden, context-specific, immensely slow and complex process.

This chapter will question the reasoning behind elevating corruption—at least as it is usually measured—to be more significant than low education, poor health, limited capacity, societal norms, or a raft of other potential barriers to rapid development. And it will suggest that the broader literature around institutional determinism is also too pessimistic. Institutions can in fact change over time scales shorter than the epochal, whatever the usual indicators may report, and weak governance (at least as common measures indicate) is not quite the end-all of development.

Corruption and Development?

It does not take a detailed look at Transparency International's Corruption Perceptions Index to work out what type of countries are thought to be particularly corrupt by the political-risk analysts, aid-agency economists, and think-tank staff members whose opinions it reflects. At the (virtuous) top of the ranking are rich countries: Sweden at number 3, the United Kingdom at 14, and the United States at 19. Toward the (villainous) bottom are poor countries: Ivory Coast at 136, Vietnam at 116, and Tanzania at 111. That developing countries are comparatively corrupt is an unquestioned truth among politicians, businesspeople, and aid-agency staff members across the West. Moreover, this corruption is widely seen as a big reason, if not the key reason, why poor countries are poor.

Yet as the previous chapter's analysis shows, it is difficult to measure corruption. It takes on many forms. And it is far easier to measure outcomes. Herein, therefore, lies the question: are our measures of corruption closely related to progress on those outcomes? The answer, broadly, is no.

The relationship between bribe levels or perceptions of corruption and growth over the first decade of the 21st century hardly jumps out of the data. Some cross-country studies find a link between higher corruption indicators and lower economic growth,[1] but measures such as Transparency International's CPI and the Worldwide Governance Indicators (WGI) are weakly correlated with measured growth outcomes. In fact, a recent analysis of 41 different studies involving 460 estimates of that impact shows that more than 60 percent could find no significant relationship between corruption and growth, while 6 percent actually suggest that more corrupt countries grew faster.[2] (Figures 3-1 and 3-2 show a similar result, with countries with higher indicators of corruption experiencing higher rates of growth.) To quote the 2015 UK Department for International Development (DFID) evidence paper on corruption, "[t]he effect of corruption on macroeconomic growth remains contested, and corruption has not been a determining factor constraining growth."[3]

It is important to emphasize four caveats: First, the evidence is weak that corruption as measured is a significant drag on economic growth across all

---

1 Svensson (2005); and Ugur and Dasgupta (2011).

2 Campos, Dimova, and Saleh (2010).

3 Menocal and others (2015, p. 7).

Figure 3-1. The Weak Link between Bribe Prevalence and Growth

GDP per capita growth (2000-10)

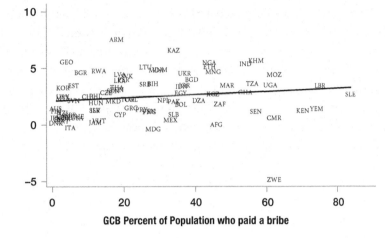

GCB Percent of Population who paid a bribe

Source: Transparency International Global Corruption Barometer and World Bank World Development Indicators.

Figure 3-2. The Weak Link between Control of Corruption and Growth

GDP per capita growth (2000-10)

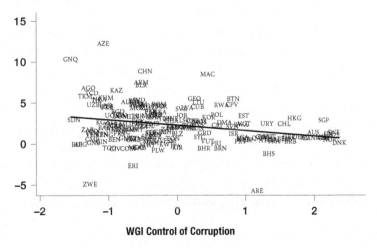

WGI Control of Corruption

Source: Transparency International Global Corruption Barometer and World Bank World Development Indicators.

countries, but it may still be a force for slower growth in particular circumstances.[4] Second, whatever its impact on average incomes, corruption is a negative outcome in its own right—people should not have to pay bribes for services or to avoid police harassment, and politicians should not get rich on kickbacks. Third, the DFID evidence paper quoted above suggests stronger links between general corruption measures and inequality, service provision, investment, and tax revenues among other outcomes.[5] And fourth, the general measures of corruption used in these analyses have significant weakness discussed in the previous chapter. Better measures of corruption might show stronger links with other outcomes. And one piece of evidence supporting such an interpretation is that measures of inequality do appear to be significantly linked with slower growth.[6]

To elaborate, it is likely that the impact of corruption depends on other factors and changes from one context to another. Mushtaq Khan from the School of Oriental and African Studies, University of London, has argued, for instance, that in some states corruption may act as a mechanism to allow the resource transfers that sustain political stability.[7] The "greasing the wheels" argument for corruption has received some empirical support in overregulated, institutionally weak settings. Pierre-Guillaume Méon from the Université libre de Bruxelles and Laurent Weill from the University of Strasbourg suggest that countries with poor regulation see higher productivity when corruption increases, while countries with effective regulation see the reverse result.[8] Again, different kinds of corruption are likely to have different economic impacts. Such conditional effects would reduce the overall strength of the relationship between measures of corruption and growth even if corruption really were growth inhibiting under most circumstances. In short, the evidence suggests that corruption (as measured) is an important factor in development outcomes, but probably is not an overwhelming one. It is no more significant and deeply causal than other factors such as learning outcomes or quality infrastructure.

Micro-level evidence also shows a weak relationship between both perceptions and surveyed petty corruption levels in infrastructure and infra-

---

4 Ugur and Dasgupta (2011).

5 Menocal and others (2015, p. 7).

6 Berg and Osrty (2013).

7 Khan (2012).

8 Méon and Weill (2008).

structure outcomes. There is some evidence linking outcomes such as the frequency of power outages to corruption measures such as Transparency International's CPI.[9] Similarly, a general measure of perceived country-level corruption is associated with lower energy use. But it is also *positively* associated with other infrastructure measures while access to water is not correlated either way.[10] Transparency International's CPI is not significantly related to any of a set of 12 infrastructure outcomes, including levels of investment, extent of access to infrastructure services, telecoms waiting lists, and transmission distribution losses.[11] Meanwhile, the surveyed extent of petty corruption in utility provision is only significantly negatively correlated with the percentage of the population with access to water, with no effect on electricity or telecoms access.[12] Corruption, as reflected by perception measures or bribe payments, is not a major barrier to the provision of infrastructure services.

Again, enterprises in developing countries do not report corruption as one of the most significant challenges they face. Of all firms surveyed by the World Bank (73,108 firms across 123 countries), only 6.2 percent selected corruption as the most serious obstacle out of the 15 possible answers (see table 3-1).[13] Corruption was the most common answer in less than 1 percent of countries and among the top three in only one in seven countries. Compare that to access to finance, ranked first in 29 percent of countries, or electricity, the top concern in more than one out of five countries. Across countries, corruption ranked eighth out of the 15 obstacles, equal with customs, trade regulation, and labor regulations. That put it below crime and disorder, political instability, informal-sector competition, tax rates, and an inadequately educated workforce.[14]

---

9 Tanzi and Davoodi (1998).

10 Estache, Goicoechea, and Trujillo (2006). These results, positive and negative alike, are open to all of the usual concerns with econometric exercises regarding questions of causality and the stability of coefficients in the presence of multicolinearity and omitted variables

11 Kenny (2006).

12 Ibid. The percentage of company managers ranking corruption as a major constraint to doing business is correlated with the percentage of managers who see electricity as a major constraint. At the same time greater concern with corruption is *positively* associated with mobile phone access and insignificantly related to other variables.

13 World Bank Group, n.d., "Enterprise Surveys," www.enterprisesurveys.org.

14 For governance: Ramachandran, Leo, and Thuotte (2011) analyze business environment surveys and conclude that the most frequently cited constraints to business in

To argue that corruption is the underlying cause of inadequate electricity or low access to finance—that the surveys misrepresent the importance of the corruption—one must assume that respondents in developing countries are ignorant of that underlying cause. Little evidence supports that assumption. Firms (and individuals) do suggest that corruption is an issue, and the evidence suggests that they are right to do so, but in the great majority of countries other issues are equally or more significant.

Institutions and Change

The argument that corruption is important to development is nested in a larger set of beliefs about the sources of overall development progress that emphasize the role of institutions. Institutions broadly defined are laws, practices, and customs—the rules of the game for social and economic interaction. More narrowly, they are about governance—the way the system works and the sort of issues reflected in both popular perceptions of corruption and academic writing by economists including Daron Acemoglu and Simon Johnson from MIT and James Robinson from the University of Chicago. And as reflected in their work, institutions are considered history-laden.

For example, some researchers argue that the social and political traits of precolonial ethnic groups that dominated particular areas of Africa may matter more to current income levels in those areas than which modern country they are found in.[15] In their landmark paper on the role of institutions in development, Acemoglu, Johnson, and Robinson focus on the colonial period itself:

> There is a variety of historical evidence . . . suggesting that the control structures set up in the non-settler colonies during the colonial era persisted, while there is little doubt that the institutions of law and order and private property established during the early phases of colonialism in Australia, Canada, New Zealand, the United

---

African fragile states are electricity, access to finance, and political instability. Corruption and tax rates come in fourth and fifth.

15 Alesina, Michalopoulos, and Papaioannou (2012).

Table 3-1. Corruption Is Not a Top Business Constraint According to World Bank Survey Data, 2006–13

Constraint	Number of firms	percentage
Access to finance	11,680	15.98
Electricity	10,078	13.79
Practices of competitors in the informal sector	9,210	12.60
Tax rates	8,548	11.69
Political instability	6,578	9.00
Inadequately educated workforce	5,514	7.54
Corruption	4,532	6.20
Crime, theft, and disorder	3,539	4.84
Labor regulations	2,437	3.33
Access to land	2,203	3.01
Tax administration	2,186	2.99
Transport	2,095	2.87
Customs and trade regulations	1,970	2.69
Business licensing and permits	1,893	2.59
Courts	645	0.88
TOTAL	73,108	

Source: World Bank Enterprise Surveys.

States, Hong Kong, and Singapore have formed the basis of the current-day institutions of these countries.[16]

Tracing through a causal chain, they argue there is "a high correlation between mortality rates faced by soldiers, bishops, and sailors in the colonies and European settlements; between European settlements and early measures of institutions; and between early institutions and institutions today."

Armed with a similar theory, Stanley Engerman from Johns Hopkins and Kenneth Sokoloff from the University of California–Los Angeles suggest that "extreme differences in the extent of inequality that arose early

---

16 Acemoglu, Johnson, and Robinson (2001)

in the history of the New World economies may have contributed to systematic differences in the ways institutions evolved." They continue by stating that "government policies [tend] to maintain the basic thrust of the initial factor endowment or the same general degree of inequality along their respective economy's path of development. . . . Systematic patterns are also seen in the character of the economic institutions that evolved in the respective societies, even after independence."[17] A recent game among economists has been to go ever further back in their search for the ultimate determinants of modern institutional forms. For example, Bill Easterly and colleagues' probing of the roots of wealth asked "Was the Wealth of Nations Determined in 1000 BC?"[18]

Modern measures of institutions also suggest strong persistence and slow change. For instance, Lant Pritchett of the Harvard Kennedy School and the Center for Global Development and colleagues argue that it would take 600 years for Haiti to reach Singapore's Government Effectiveness score on the WGI even with the most generous interpretation of its rate of progress since independence.[19] The architects of the WGI, Daniel Kaufmann of the Natural Resource Governance Institute and colleagues, themselves suggest reasons to be depressed about global prospects as a whole: "[R]eviewing the time series of the individual sources over the past several updates of the WGI, we have documented that there is very little evidence of trends over time in global averages of our individual underlying data sources."[20] It is hard not to become a little downbeat about the prospects for poor countries as a result.

History certainly does matter to present-day outcomes. Look at the stability of income rankings across 53 countries over time: the average country has moved only 10 places in the rankings over 183 years (see figure 3-3). There are outliers, with Australia and New Zealand improving dramatically and Jamaica falling precipitously, but generally speaking, being relatively rich in 1820 is a good predictor of being relatively rich in 2003.

---

17 Engerman and Sokoloff (2002, p. 35).

18 Comin, Easterly, and Gong (2010).

19 Pritchett, Woolcock, and Andrews (2010). Bill Savedoff, in review comments on this book, notes that Singapore itself would not have rated toward the top of a 1960 WGI measure, suggesting again that institutions, or at least scores on an institutional ranking, can change quite fast.

20 Kaufmann, Kraay, and Mastruzzi (2011).

Figure 3-3. Country-Income Rankings Are Generally Stable over Time

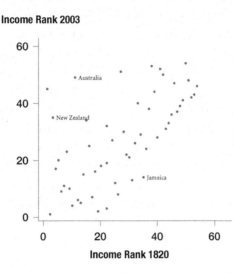

Source: Maddison database (www.ggdc.net/maddison/maddison-project/data.htm).

Institutions and Growth

But for all of the strong evidence that wealth depends on history and that institutional factors are correlated with economic growth, there is still much more to development than slow-changing historically determined institutions.[21]

First, what causes what is open to debate. In a recent review, Richard Bluhm and Adam Szirmai of the United Nations University find "strong support" that institutions are among the sources of long-term growth, but the extent to which growth causes improved institutions "remains highly debated."[22] Edward Glaeser from Harvard University and colleagues go further and suggest that human capital is the basis of development: it causes growth, which causes institutional advancement.[23]

Second, the link between perceived levels of governance and changes in

---

21 See the review in Acemoglu and Robinson (2008). See also Easterly, Ritzen, and Wool-cock (2006).

22 Bluhm and Szirmai (2012, p. 82).

23 Glaeser and others (2004). They also point out important imperfections in contempo-raneous institutional measures including that they tend to measure outcomes ("there was little expropriation") not actual institutional constraints ("the president simply could not expropriate often even should he have wanted to").

development outcomes over time is at best partial. In a 2011 study for the European Bank of Reconstruction and Development, Simon Commander and Zlatko Nikoloski conclude that democracy is not reliably associated with economic growth and that the World Bank's Doing Business and Enterprise Survey indicators are not closely linked with outcomes such as higher investment, capital inflows, or firm productivity.[24] They suggest that there is a measurement problem—most of the indicators used to measure institutions are subjective—but the issue may also be that institutions as usually defined matter less than is usually supposed.

Other cross-country studies suggest similarly fragile relationships between institutional measures and economic growth.[25] Denis de Crombrugghe and Kristine Farla of the United Nations University report, for example, that strong institutions are related to income levels but find "no such evidence on growth rates."[26] And specific case studies also suggest that there is more to current outcomes than centuries of history. Take the case of North and South Korea; both had a similar cultural and political legacy in 1945 but have taken dramatically different economic trajectories since then. And perhaps of particular relevance to this book, early studies suggesting that aid promotes economic growth only in the presence of strong institutions have not withstood the test of time, or robustness challenges.[27]

On the question of whether there is more to growth than slow-changing institutions, consider this: In the past 60 years (a blink of the eye in institution-building time), there has been consistent and historically very strong growth in per capita output across most of the world. Among countries for which the Penn World Tables (a preeminent measure of income) have data, about 5.1 billion people live in countries where average incomes have more than doubled since 1960, and 4.1 billion—well over half the planet—live in countries where average incomes have tripled or more. Nearly 2.2 billion people are in countries where average incomes

---

24 Commander and Nikoloski (2011).
25 Durlauf, Kourtellos, and Chih (2008); Glaeser and others (2004); Bazzi and Clemens (2013); Jinfeng and Yi (2015); Albouy (2008); and Jie and others (2013).
26 De Crombrugghe and Farla (2012, p. 1).
27 Roodman (2007); Minoiu and Reddy (2010); Doucouliagos and Paldam (2010); and Verspagen (2012).

have more than *quintupled* over the past 50 years. This includes the citizens of China, Japan, Egypt, and Thailand, all of whom have seen around an eightfold increase in average incomes since 1960.

Such growth has not touched all corners of the globe. About 200 million people live in nine African economies where the average income per head *declined* between 1960 and 2010. That includes the populations of Kenya and the Democratic Republic of the Congo. And about another 700 million live in countries where incomes have climbed since 1960, but where the average citizen in 2010 remained less than twice as rich as 50 years before.

But the majority of people alive today live in countries that have experienced unprecedented economic growth, even compared to the Industrial Revolution. Between 1820 and 1870, for instance, GDP per capita for the United Kingdom increased from $1,706 to $3,190—an 87 percent increase—according to data from Angus Maddison of the University of Groningen.[28] If that performance had occurred between 1960 and 2010, this growth would have placed the United Kingdom 34th lowest out of the 107 countries for which the Penn Tables have data. In other words, 73 countries, including the Philippines and Zimbabwe—rarely thought of as economic powerhouses or homes to world-class institutions—have had stronger economic growth in the past 50 years than the United Kingdom did from 1820 to 1870.

Because of all of that growth, a lot of the world is now rich by the standards of just a few decades ago. Nearly 1.7 billion people live in countries where the average income per capita was above $10,000 in 2010. That is nearly the level of the United Kingdom's GDP per capita in 1960 and above the average income in France, Germany, the Netherlands, and Belgium at the time. More than 3.5 billion people worldwide—about half the planet—live in countries with a 2010 average income of $6,000 or more, according to the Penn Tables. That is a little below the GDP per capita of Italy in 1960 and above that of Ireland or Spain in the same year.

---

28 The Maddison-Project, 2013 version, www.ggdc.net/maddison/maddison-project/home.htm.

Institutions and Non-Income Measures of Development
These improvements are not only about economic growth and affect more
than just middle-income countries: there has been dramatic improvement
across a range of different indicators. In fact, the evidence for progress on
non-income measures is even stronger. From 1950 to 1999, for example,
average global life expectancy increased from 51 to 69 years while the difference between countries narrowed (the standard deviation fell from 13
to 7 years).[29]

All this improvement means one of two things. Either the quality of
life that people experience under low-quality governance today is the same
as the quality of life found under high-quality governance in 1950, or *average* governance has improved since 1950 so that countries like Brazil
and South Africa are as well governed today as countries like the United
Kingdom and Canada were in 1950.[30] So which is it? There is evidence
for both—some data point to better performance from improving institutions, and some point to better performance despite lack of such improvement. Tables 3-2 through 3-4 help illustrate these connected performance
improvements.

Table 3-2 aggregates country data into quartiles based on the countries'
governance-effectiveness rankings in the 2011 Worldwide Governance Indicators, and compares the average development outcomes achieved by
each quartile over time. In the second quartile of governance quality GDP
per capita in 1950 was $1,365. By 2011, it was $5,754. Infant mortality in
those countries also improved, dropping from 12.6 percent to 4 percent
over that time. Similarly, looking at countries divided into quartiles based
on their settler mortality in colonial times, the second (worse) quartile
settler mortality predicted GDP in 1950 was $1,867; it had risen to $5,550
by 2011. Second quartile settler mortality predicted infant mortality
dropped from 13 percent to 5.6 percent over that period. Both results suggest that either institutions have become considerably stronger since 1950
or the same quality of institutions is associated with far better outcomes.
Which is it? The tables suggest better outcomes at a given level of reported
governance/mortality when applied to an institutional measure for which
we have data going back to 1950: the Polity II measure of democracy. This
measure runs from -10 (fully autocratic) to 10 (fully democratic). The

---

29 Kenny (2005).
30 Ibid.

second quartile score on polity based on setter mortality has climbed from -0.6 in 1950 to 5.8 in 2011. This improvement, especially pronounced since the end of the Cold War,[31] suggests that better outcomes may be coming from better institutions.

Tables 3-3 and 3-4, however, suggest that better outcomes are emerging even without commensurate improvements in institutions. Table 3-3 lists the 13 richest countries in 1950 and their GDP, government effectiveness ranks, infant mortality rates, and Polity scores. Table 3-4 does the same for countries that fell within the same range of GDP in 2011. Gabon and Panama, for instance, had a GDP per capita in 2011 similar to what Australia and Switzerland had in 1950. All of the richest countries in 1950 still score very high on government effectiveness and scored a perfect 10 on Polity's democracy measure in 1950. The countries with similar GDP in 2011 show, with considerably more variance, far lower 2011 government effectiveness and Polity scores alongside lower (better) infant mortality rates. In this sample, the same income is associated with lower democracy and better infant mortality in 2011 than in 1950.

With some evidence of institutional improvement over time and some evidence that outcomes have improved at the same level of institutional quality, the picture is perhaps blurry, but at least it is broadly positive. This should be no surprise since *institutions* covers a range of different things, from constitutions to company and financial structures to electoral rules and methods of educational curriculum design. The concept overlaps heavily with norms and culture. It may be that some types of institution can change more rapidly than other types, that some depend more on context than others, and that the relative importance of different institutions to outcomes changes over time.

Institutions Can Change Quickly
To provide some micro bones to this macro analysis, there are in fact examples of fairly rapid institutional change, as noted by Acemoglu, Johnson, and Robinson in their paper on colonial influences on modern institutions: "It is useful to point out that our findings do not imply that institutions today are predetermined by colonial policies and cannot be changed. . . . In fact, our reading is that these results suggest substantial

---

31 Kenny (2008).

Table 3-2. Same Institutions, Better Outcomes?

Government effectiveness quartile	GDP Per Capita ($USPPP)		Infant mortality rate (%)		Polity score	
	1950	2011	1950	2011	1950	2011
First	2,060	3,596	16.8	7.7	−3.72	0.30
Second	1,365	5,754	12.6	4.0	−3.39	2.77
Third	2,636	11,840	10.0	2.0	−0.68	5.93
Fourth	6,866	35,395	4.8	0.6	6.50	8.12

Sources: Penn World Tables, Abouharb and Kimball (2007), Polity Database.

Table 3-3. The Richest Countries in 1950 All Had Strong Institutions

1950	GDP per Capita (U.S.$PPP)	Government effectiveness rank	Infant mortality rate (%)	Polity score
United States	12,668	88.6	3.6	10
Switzerland	12,536	97.6	3.1	10
Australia	11,756	95.3	2.4	10
New Zealand	10,602	98.1	2.8	10
Luxembourg	10,550	94.8	4.6	10
Canada	9,739	97.2	4.2	10
Denmark	8,227	99.5	3.1	10
Sweden	8,221	98.6	2.1	10
United Kingdom	7,749	92.4	3.5	10
Norway	7,724	96.2	2.8	10
Iceland	7,116	92.9	2.2	
Belgium	7,083	93.8	5.3	10
Netherlands	6,280	96.7	2.5	10

Sources: Penn World Tables, Abouharb and Kimball (2007), Polity Database.

Table 3-4. Countries Today as Wealthy as the Richest Countries in
1950 Have Weaker Institutions

2011	GDP (US$PPP)	Government effectiveness rank	Infant mortality rate (%)	Polity score
Gabon	12,201	19.4	6.5	3
Panama	12,012	58.8	1.9	9
Botswana	11,519	68.2	5.6	8
Dominica	11,299	70.1	1.3	
Venezuela	10,218	13.3	1.6	−3
Costa Rica	10,094	64.0	10.1	10
Maldives	9,992	44.1	1.2	
Mauritius	9,501	74.4	1.5	10
Brazil	9,205	55.5	1.5	8
Equatorial Guinea	8,962	3.3	10.4	−5
Peru	8,812	49.3	1.9	9
Dominican Republic	8,698	34.6	2.8	8
Grenada	8,422	61.6	1.4	
South Africa	8,368	64.9	4.7	9
Thailand	8,360	59.7	1.4	7
Colombia	8,311	62.6	1.8	7
China	7,827	60.7	1.5	−7
Belize	7,333	43.1	1.9	
Ecuador	6,732	35.1	2.4	5
Suriname	6,588	51.7	2.1	5

Sources: Penn World Tables, World Bank World Development Indicators, Polity Database.

economic gains from improving institutions, for example as in the case of Japan during the Meiji Restoration or South Korea during the 1960s."[32]

Take the case of reforming utilities as another example. Phnom Penh has improved the quality and reach of its water supply with the introduction of market pricing and a decline in nonrevenue water (which was sent through the pipes but not paid for) from 72 percent to 6 percent, intro-

---

32 Acemoglu, Johnson, and Robinson (2001, p. 1395).

duced between 1993 and 2009. Piped water coverage increased over that period from 40 percent of the city to more than 90 percent in 2009, while water service increased from an average of 10 hours a day to 24.[33] The institutions connected with the water authority, including new regulations and the enforcement of billing, clearly developed quite rapidly. Or look at leakage of the financial variety: the percentage of central government financing for equipment in Ugandan schools that actually reaches the schools has increased from next to nothing to next to everything over the past 10 years, after newspapers published how much money the schools were meant to get.[34]

Even the attitudes that underlie institutions can rapidly adjust. For example, in India the Dalits (or "untouchables," the lowest of India's castes) have been subject to widespread discrimination for millennia and have had access only to a narrow range of jobs thought of as unclean. But a survey designed and led by members of the Dalit community in two areas of Uttar Pradesh found that attitudes and behaviors related to the low status of Dalits had been widely tempered or abandoned over the past 20 years.[35] Dalit respondents report that, since 1990, they are far more likely to sit next to high-caste guests at weddings rather than being seated separately, they are no longer expected to handle the dead animals of other castes, and non-Dalit midwives will attend births in Dalit households. They have moved in large numbers into nontraditional professions such as tailoring and driving, and almost none participate in bonded labor for high-caste patrons.

The changes are huge. In Bulandshahar District, less than 4 percent of Dalits said that non-Dalits would accept food in their household in 1990, but nearly half said that they would today. In 1990, 73 percent of respondents suggested that only Dalits would have handled dead animals; that number fell to 1 in 20 in 2007. Dalits were considerably wealthier in 2007 than they were in 1990. The proportion with a television in Bulandshahar climbed from less than 1 percent to nearly 50 percent, and bicycle ownership rose from around one-third to more than four-fifths. The researchers suggest that the social transformation is far too dramatic to be accounted for by income changes alone.

---

33 Das and others (2010).
34 Reinikka and Svensson (2002).
35 Kapur and others (2010).

If institutions and their cultural underpinnings can change rapidly, so can the necessity of strong institutions to development progress. New technologies can reduce the effect of poor institutions. Take the case of the mobile phone. In countries as ill-governed or ungoverned as Somalia, the new technology allowed for the competitive provision of phone services. With far fewer institutional requirements than landlines, and considerably lower costs of infrastructure, mobile phones became available to more than 5 billion people worldwide in only about two decades.

A similar decline in the effect of poor institutions has occurred in health. In the age before vaccines, bed nets, and antibiotics, improving health outcomes required considerable public works and sanitation programs: piped water and sewage, garbage collection, close monitoring of food production, and so on. Although these approaches are still effective today, mortality and morbidity rates can be considerably reduced with far cheaper and more straightforward vaccination campaigns and pill delivery.[36] Again, it is clear that history matters, and that institutions matter to the quality of life and to health care in particular. That only 1 percent of Chad's nonwage health budget officially allocated to frontline clinics actually reaches them has a real impact on the quality of care—and on health—in the country. And improved government service provision alongside private-sector regulation will become increasingly important as health care providers turn from the most basic challenges (infectious disease) and move on to more complex areas (cancer). But still, there is more to life than strong governance, and—perhaps even better news— weak governance is neither unfixable nor an insurmountable obstacle to progress.

Conclusion

The popular perception of corruption discussed in chapter 2 was a broader "system stacked" notion that fits better with the views of institutional scholars as to where the problem of development lies. This popular perception has more to recommend it empirically than a quid pro quo definition in terms of explaining outcomes.

---

36 Kenny (2011).

The good news is that the evidence suggests even this broader sense of corruption is not the be-all and end-all of development. The Enterprise Surveys discussed in this chapter suggest that firms believe that lack of capital, poor-quality education, and bad policy choices are more important than corruption as the determinants of their performance. Perhaps they prefer the older explanations for why poor countries are poor over the new institutional economics. And they may well have a point: while historically determined institutions do appear to have a role in explaining which countries are relatively rich or relatively poor, relatively healthy or relatively sick, clearly there is a lot more to development progress than (static) institutions alone.

Governance writ large is clearly necessary to produce relative prosperity and a decent quality of life. No country is peaceful and rich without a functioning legal and regulatory system or public services that provide infrastructure and education. But governance is not the sole preserve of those on the right side of a historical divide. Corruption is a barrier to development, but not such an overwhelming one that any policy or any price is worth paying in the fight to control it. Because corruption is only one of many barriers to development, ill-designed or cumbersome efforts to fight it can themselves be a drag on development prospects. The next chapters discuss how to avoid that trap.

4

Improving Institutions

Between 2003 and 2007, Nuhu Ribadu was chair of Nigeria's Economic and Financial Crimes Commission. During that time, Ribadu investigated Nigerian government officials who had been bribed by the U.S. firm Kellogg, Brown, and Root in connection with a liquefied natural gas plant contract; convicted the inspector general of police of embezzlement; and recorded the governor of Nigeria's Delta State offering him a $15 million bribe to end his investigations.[1] He also survived an assassination attempt. These investigations demonstrate not only the bravery of Ribadu and his team but also just how significant corruption is to development in Nigeria. Police, anticorruption bodies, and courts have a central role to play in controlling corruption and bringing the corrupt to justice—people who steal millions and sometimes billions in public finances should be arrested and locked up.

Sadly, the performance record of anticorruption agencies in particular is mixed. Often they are a greater part of the problem than the solution, as Nigeria's former inspector general of police was. Absent a hero like Ribadu, their deterrent role may often be limited.[2] The same can be true even with such a hero—when an ally of the Delta State governor was elected president in 2007, Ribadu was sacked, and the governor walked free.

---

1 Kennedy (2010).

2 Meagher (2002).

Anticorruption agencies are not the only ones at fault. The track record of measures specifically designed to counter corruption, especially in more corrupt countries, is patchy and contradictory. Jesper Johnsøn and Nils Taxell from the U4 Anti-Corruption Resource Center and Dominik Zaum of the University of Reading, in their review of "evidence gaps" regarding what works in anticorruption, suggest that the gaps are larger than the evidence. They argue that the only anticorruption interventions shown to work are public financial management measures, in particular publishing budgets down to the final recipient. Half of all interventions they review have mixed or contested results, and evidence for the other half is weak.[3] Take, for example, one suggested response to corruption: raise salaries so officials will not feel the need to ask for bribes and will be more worried about losing their jobs if they do. This proposal makes sense, but when Ghana doubled police salaries in 2010, the officers patrolling Ghana's roads ended up receiving more bribes from truckers, not fewer.[4]

Given the evidence shown in the previous chapters about the complexities of measuring corruption, it should come as little surprise that in many cases the evidence about what works to reduce corruption is weak. But this weak evidence suggests that evaluators should focus on approaches that improve outcomes (which can be measured), rather than practices (which cannot). A greater focus on outcomes can reduce corruption and improve governance.[5] And the good news of the previous chapters is that institutional change can be rapid and have a significant impact on outcomes in the right circumstances—there is real hope for progress.

---

3 Johnsøn, Taxell, and Zaum (2012).

4 Foltz and Opoju-Agyemang (2015). More broadly, the link between governance reforms including greater overall democratization or decentralization and reduced (perceptions of) corruption is weak. See Menocal and others (2015).

5 It also suggests the wisdom of Shah and Schacter's (2004) conclusion that "because corruption is itself a symptom of fundamental governance failure, the higher the incidence of corruption, the *less* an anticorruption strategy should include tactics that are narrowly targeted at corrupt behavior and the *more* it should focus on the broad underlying features of the governance environment" (42). The UK Department of Finance and International Development Evidence Paper on corruption similarly suggests that "[a]nticorruption measures are most effective when other contextual factors support them and when they are integrated into a broader package of institutional reforms" (Menocal and others 2015, p. 7).

Deregulation, Competition, and Simplification

At the heart of anticorruption efforts, and central to the efficient provision of government services, is reducing the gap between what governments pay for services and what those services actually cost to provide. This "rent" makes space for corrupt payouts or theft. Deregulating, introducing competition, and simplifying procedures can be powerful tools to reduce those rents. However, there are caveats. First, a lot of regulation is absolutely necessary. It may be true that if there were no government, there would be no government corruption, but this is not a price worth paying. Second, changing the public role from delivering goods and services to regulating private delivery still requires strong government oversight. Reforms tend to be partial solutions at best, and they always depend on specific contexts. Governments need to measure results, evaluate whether a reform is having the desired effect, and adjust their policies accordingly.

The potential impact of removing unnecessary regulation on corruption can be demonstrated by the history of Jakarta's water supply. In the late 1980s, only 14 percent of the city's population lived in households connected to the municipal water system. One-third of people in Indonesia's capital relied on water from street vendors. They paid between three and fifty times as much for water as did people with a household connection. Water vendors got their supplies from public taps, of which there were very few—just 1,200 serving at least 2.5 million people. This increased the labor costs of the street vendors, who usually transported water using jerricans piled on handcarts. Nonetheless, the vendors were earning hourly wages two to three times the average for men with primary or lower education. The public taps were controlled by operators who, in turn, charged three to six times their costs for water per liter.

Why were these water prices so much higher than any reasonable calculation of labor costs and wholesale prices suggested that they should be? And why were there so few public taps? It was not that the cost of construction was out of reach: 5,000 to 10,000 additional taps could have been constructed for less than the price of one of the city's underutilized water-treatment plants. It appears that the street vendors were running a cartel, supported by bribes to local officials and employees of the water utility. After subtracting the costs of labor, equipment, and payments to tap operators, nearly half of the price paid to vendors for water by households was accounted for by cartel rents and bribes. In turn, after accounting for official payments to the utility for water and operating costs, about 60 percent of vendor payments to tap operators were available for excess profit and bribe payments. And it appeared that the number of public taps had been optimized to maximize the rents available for water vendors and utility staff.

The solution eventually adopted by the Jakarta government was simple: allow any householder with a tap to sell water. That introduced competition to the cartel and forced prices paid by consumers toward the actual cost of service provision. As a result of that simple move, water prices paid by unconnected households dropped between 30 and 60 percent. [6]

A lot of well-meaning regulation the world over fails to achieve its objectives. There is no correlation across countries, for example, between the number of procedures required to get permission to build a warehouse and the number of accidents involving workers.[7] Weak enforcement or inadequate rules may be to blame, but even then these are grounds to reconsider regulatory design. Countries should pare back regulations to those that have the highest social value and that can be fairly and effectively enforced. Easing the process of regulatory compliance will also help reduce governance failure, through approaches such as consolidated clearances and pro-applicant time limits (whereby licenses not issued or denied within a certain period are automatically granted).

Yet regulatory simplification is by no means a guaranteed path to riches through reduced corruption. Countries that have reduced the number of steps to complete official regulatory processes have seen an increase in the amount of time that it actually takes for firms to follow procedures, according to analysis by Mary Hallward-Driemeier from the World Bank and Lant Pritchett of the Harvard Kennedy School and Center for Global Development. Again, analysis of Enterprise Surveys by Pritchett, Hallward-Dreimer, and their colleague Gita Khun Jush suggests that firms do better with more regulation consistently enforced than less regulation enforced by a capricious bureaucrat.[8] In turn, the problem of regulation enforcement may be one reason why it is hard to find a strong relationship between rankings on the World Bank's Doing Business surveys of the de

---

6 Lovei and Whittington (1991).

7 See Djankov and others (2000) for a broader discussion of the limited impact of regulation of entry on quality of service provision, but its stronger link with the extent of corruption, across a range of sectors.

8 Hallward-Driemeier, Jush, and Pritchett (2010).

jure complexity of business regulations and broad development outcomes. China is 87 places behind the United States in the rankings, and yet China was able to more than double the size of its economy over the past 10 years. In that same period, higher rankings also did not stop the United States from falling into recession.

Still, the burdens surveyed, however imperfectly by Doing Business, do matter. In countries with weak oversight and management of regulatory bodies, more regulation all too often means more bribery and delay rather than better (safer, more economically efficient) outcomes. Cutting down regulation is likely to mean less institutional failure, lower petty bribery, and somewhat better outcomes. What is important for reduced corruption and increased efficiency is ensuring that the de jure regulations are necessary, straightforward, and universally applied.

Similar lessons apply at the sectoral level in infrastructure, education, and health—deregulation and competition, where they can be applied, can help, but beware the expectation of miracles.[9] Even apparently well-regulated private fixed-line telecom monopolies in developing countries are languishing, for example. Between 2005 and 2011, the number of fixed-phone subscribers dropped from 12.5 to 11 percent of the developing world's population. In the same period, the number of mobile subscriptions more than tripled—climbing from 22 percent to 77 percent of the developing world. Mobile telephony involving regulated private competition, though hardly completely corruption-free, has worked where private monopolies have not.[10] Without competition, privatization has made little difference to telecommunications provision.

Katharina Gassner from the World Bank and colleagues, in the most comprehensive analysis of private and public provision of water and electricity in developing countries carried out to date, report that greater participation by private firms is associated with an increase in quality as measured by the length of uninterrupted daily supply, an improvement in collection rates, a decline in operational losses (by between one-tenth and one-third in electricity), improved labor productivity, and an expanded

---

9 Rossotto and others (2004) find that international calls in fully competitive international markets cost 66 percent less than those in countries with partial competition. Prices for a basket of fixed telecommunications services are 20 percent lower in developing countries with competition than countries where there is a monopoly in provision (World Bank 2005).

10 See, for example, the scandal of 2G license corruption in India (Magnier 2010).

capital base.[11] At the same time, the results on service price and infrastructure rollout were inconclusive, meaning that liberalization and privatization were no guarantee of access and affordability. And, regardless, the introduction of private provision, especially absent competition, requires high-quality governance in both the initial privatization and the regulation of providers. Privatization may simply change the nature of corruption and rent seeking from one of extracting rents on service provision to one of steering license or utility acquisition and regulatory compliance.[12]

Or take education: According to internationally comparable test scores, Chile improved student learning at the fastest rate worldwide between 1995 and 2011. The country combined a system of publicly funded school choice and increased autonomy to headmasters with teacher assessment and a national all-student assessment testing regime. Despite that improvement, considerable gaps still remain between performance in the best and worst schools, and students from richer families benefited from the move to the voucher system more than those from poor families.[13]

Similarly, a recent analysis of a program that provided vouchers to

---

11 Gassner, Popov, and Pushak (2007).

12 Andres, Guasch, and Straub (2007) find that regulators in Latin America that were established under law, were well funded by regulatory levy, and had a fixed-term regulatory commission screened by legislators were considerably better at aligning cost of capital and rate of return. Gasmi, Noumba Um, and Virto (2006) find that independent regulation financed from operator contributions produces better outcomes in telecoms in terms of network rollout. Despite these findings, a survey of regulators in 2005 found that less than 30 percent of regulators currently publish contracts and licenses (Bertolini 2006). Seventy-one percent of East Asian regulators disclosed procedures and decisions, while 42 percent disclosed licenses and contracts, in a 2004 survey (Muzzini 2006). Gassner, Popov, and Pushak (2007) find that the impact of the mere presence of a regulator is muted, suggesting the need for considerable institution-building beyond legal authorization. Furthermore, there is evidence that the independent regulatory model may be inappropriate at least in some sectors in smaller economies, suggesting the need for alternate approaches that combine transparency with limited discretion (Ehrhardt and others 2007). The potential role for private infrastructure provision also appears limited in many sectors. Across infrastructure as a whole, governments and donors still account for around four-fifths of sector investment. It is worth comparing estimated annual investment needs for energy, transport, water, and sanitation infrastructure in developing countries of $131 billion a year to private investment commitments in those sectors in developing countries estimated at $35 billion in 2005. See Fay and Yepes (2003) on investment needs.

13 Bravo, Mukhopadhya, and Todd (2010).

pay for private schooling in the Indian state of Andhra Pradesh found that the voucher schools provided education at one-third of the cost of public schools while achieving better test results.[14] But the results from the Andhra Pradesh study also suggest the limits to an analysis based purely on public or private provision. The voucher students scored better than their contemporaries in public schools, but this is compared to a grim average: only a little more than half of all children in fifth grade in the state can read a second-grade text.[15] Public or private, learning outcomes in Andhra Pradesh are truly atrocious compared to those achieved by the average student in a U.S. or European school. The role of different institutional models of schooling systems across countries is secondary.

Many of the same lessons regarding the role of competition also apply to government tendering—fierce competition is desirable where it will work, but it does not always work. Anh Tran from Indiana University Bloomington gained access to the internal records of a firm in an East Asian country and found that bribes paid by the firm totaled an average of 15 percent of contract values when no auction was required, 24 percent of contract values when an auction based on a combination of cost and (subjective) quality was used, and 11 percent when lowest price was used as the sole criterion for all qualifying firms.[16] But while competitive lowest-price auctions may provide the lowest rents for bribes or the least opportunity to make bribes, price-only auctions are not always the best model, as suggested by experience in the private sector. From 1995 to 2000, almost half of private-sector nonresidential building construction projects in northern California were procured using negotiations. Only 18 percent were procured using unrestricted open-competitive bidding. Empirical analysis suggests that auctions are rarer in the private sector when projects are complex, contractual design is incomplete, or there are few available bidders.[17] And in corrupt regimes, even successful procurement competition may merely shift where corruption takes place, from bribing to win the contract at a high price to bribing to cover up substandard works. Mea-

---

14 Woodhead, Frost, and James (2013).
15 Pratham USA, n.d., "Andhra Pradesh," http://prathamusa.org/regions/andhra-pradesh.
16 Tran (2008).
17 Bajari, McMillan, and Tadelis (2009).

sures of competition that do not take quality into account do not work as a method to guarantee development impact.

Reducing the complexity of government service provision is another method to reduce the opportunity for funds to go astray. Technology-assisted simplification is helping to reduce leakage in India's safety-net programs, for example. The country's universal biometric ID system (based on fingerprints and iris scans) is being used to provide secure identification for new bank customers opening an account under the government's People Money Scheme (Jan Dhan Yojana). Between August 2014 and March 2015 alone, more than 135 million new accounts were opened. And using those accounts, India is moving from a system of subsidizing goods from food through fuel, housing, and education to providing cash payments into bank accounts instead.

Subsidy payments in India total about $280 billion a year—more than 4 percent of the country's GDP according to the government.[18] These subsidies are incredibly inefficient, both in terms of targeting poor people and because a lot of the subsidized goods are lost to corruption and mishandling. The $15 billion kerosene subsidy program loses 40 percent of subsidized gas to "leakage," and less than half of what is left actually flows to households in poverty. The Indian government has started moving away from subsidies toward direct payments: more than 100 million households in the country that used to have the right to buy subsidized cooking fuel have traded that right for a cash transfer into their bank account.[19] That will save the government as much as $6.5 billion a year in leakage.

The broad lesson of deregulation, competition, and simplification is that they can sometimes help but are far from corruption (or inefficiency) cure-alls. Additional techniques are important, including those to empower the multiple people who are involved in investment, operation, regulation, and use of government services to spot and report substandard work or corruption perceptions.

---

18 Pratham USA, "Andhra Pradesh."
19 *Times of India* (2015).

Information and Transparency

Audits can inflate minor transgressions of financial management or procurement rules into red flags of corruption that are used as grounds for halting projects, as with the case of the U.S. Special Inspector General for Afghanistan Reconstruction in chapter 1. But when used correctly, as a tool to track how resources are flowing and if they are successfully used for their intended purposes, audits are a vital part of a system that focuses on development results and can increase efficiency and reduce waste. In the hospitals of Buenos Aires, for example, prices of medications dropped 12 percent when procurement monitoring was increased.[20]

Any system that allows for scaled-up audits that automatically track finances through to outcomes will be particularly powerful. In Andhra Pradesh, electrical transmission and distribution losses were reduced from 38 to 26 percent from 1999 to 2003 in large part through metering and the regularization of 2.25 million unauthorized connections.[21] Nigeria biometrically enrolled all of its federal staff and eliminated 43,000 ghost workers from the payrolls as a result. A biometric audit in the country also reduced the number of federal pensioners by almost 40 percent by weeding out fraudulent beneficiaries. When Botswana moved its pension and grants registration to a biometric system, the number of recipients fell by one-quarter thanks to the removal of duplicates, ghosts, and the deceased.[22]

Transparency further amplifies the impact of improved information on financial flows and results. It is, in effect, a tool to allow anyone to audit. Transparency can provide the data required for other parts of government as well as firms, citizens, and the media to track how money is spent and what the government gets for that money. Publishing the federal financing meant to reach individual schools in Ugandan newspapers, as discussed in chapter 2, is an example of that role. Transparency through to final delivery allows citizens to know they got what they paid for and act on the results. In Brazil, when the federal government published audits of municipal expenditure of federal funds, mayors who were found to have

---

20 Di Tella and Schargrodsky (2003).

21 Gulati and Rao (2006).

22 Gelb and Clark (2013).

misspent the funds were significantly less likely to be reelected, especially where there were local radio stations to publicize the audit results.[23]

Transparency can also help minimize malfeasance in politics. Around one-third of countries worldwide require politicians to publish financial and conflict-of-interest information.[24] A bureaucrat or elected official who suddenly becomes richer while in office or soon thereafter is a "result" worth tracking. On the contracting side, Colombia's e-procurement website regularly publishes the full contract for procured goods and services, along with contract amendments and extensions and a range of other documents from the procurement process to final evaluation. In 2008, the site was already getting nearly half a million visitors a month.

Colombia is not alone. The United Kingdom, Slovakia, Georgia, and the state of Minas Gerais in Brazil have followed a similar path for some or all of their contracts. Contract publication in Slovakia, with broader openness around contracting opportunities and the procurement system in general, has raised the average number of bids on government tenders by one to two bidders, and there is mounting anecdotal evidence that the system has improved value for money as well.[25] And a World Bank–financed infrastructure project in Bali, Indonesia, that combined publishing details on contracting and project progress with audit and complaint mechanisms reduced prices for goods and works by 21 percent compared to contracts with less disclosure.

Even with clear micro evidence of the advantages of transparency and oversight mechanisms, they do have limitations. India's Annual Status of Education Report (ASER) conducts half a million assessments of literacy and numeracy in a representative set of households countrywide. The results, which are widely publicized and subject of intense debate, suggest that nearly one-half of fifth-grade students cannot read a second-grade text and one-fifth cannot follow a first-grade text. But ASER survey data from 2006 to 2012 show that more states are declining in student performance than improving. If data on learning outcomes were enough to change the situation, the trend should have been in the opposite direction, especially since school funding over that time rose dramatically.[26] Again, despite considerable de jure powers

---

23 Ferraz and Finan (2009).

24 Djankov and others (2009).

25 Center for Global Development Working Group on Contract Publication (2014).

26 Results for Development Institute (2015).

of oversight by village education committees in the Indian state of Uttar Pradesh and efforts to increase interest in and awareness of schooling quality and the role of village education committees, schooling outcomes remain poor in the state and village education committees are dysfunctional.[27]

There can also be considerable costs associated with additional transparency and oversight. The World Bank–financed Indonesia Urban Poverty Program, which disbursed about $100 million a year to more than 8,000 villages, provides one example of both benefits and costs. As part of the oversight mechanism, 100,000 elected volunteers served as project overseers. In addition, a website included individual project details, implementation and disbursement statuses, full consultant contracts, consultant invoices, details on travel expenses related to the project, and a complaint-handling mechanism.[28] The website was visited more than 2,000 times a day and recorded 6,423 complaints in 2007. Eighty-four of these complaints involved misuse of funds totaling $80,000. As a result of the complaints, a court action was launched and $32,000 in funds has been returned. At the same time, the total cost of capacity building and oversight mechanisms was estimated at 13 percent of project costs, or a little more than $24 million out of a $186 million project. These costs are lower than the benefits frequently associated with oversight and transparency in community projects, and many are one-off expenditures associated with benefits that will far outlast the life of the project, but they are still considerable.

These examples suggest that informed consumers need the power (and motivation) to respond to or fix problems revealed by increased transparency. And because of their costs, transparency and information exercises should, as much as possible, use and enhance existing reporting mechanisms rather than create bespoke project- or process-specific systems.

A further caveat regards the impact on public attitudes toward corruption and trust in government. Because popular concern over political corruption appears to be distantly related to service quality or even levels of bribe payments, it would be optimistic to assume that even a very successful strategy of institutional reform that improved outcomes and reduced corruption would necessarily have an impact on public attitudes about the extent of that corruption—let alone expert perception

---

27 Banerjee and others (2008).
28 Soraya (2009).

measures. The converse is also true, of course: shifting popular or expert perceptions should not be taken as the measure of a successful anticorruption strategy.

Focusing on Outputs and Outcomes

Minimizing the damage done by corruption involves countering the incentives to hire, buy, or build the wrong thing and to operate it badly. If this is our concern, we should focus attention on macrosectoral issues such as overall budgeting and investment selection and on auditing of outcomes. If governments are hiring the right people, buying the right resources, and using those people and resources effectively, the impact of corruption on overall development will be comparatively small and its extent will be limited. Public expenditure-tracking surveys, physical audits, and consumer surveys are key tools for measuring corruption and for gauging whether goods and services are being delivered efficiently. These tools can be complemented by asset declarations and audits of senior government officials as other measures of outcomes.

Rather than relying on perceptions or expert intuition, governance measures that rely on inputs and outputs can use objective indicators. Take the existing good benchmarks for the cost of maintaining different classes of roads, for example. Is the government budgeting adequate resources to fully maintain the road network according to those benchmarks? With regard to outputs, it is a comparatively simple engineering task to determine through a physical audit if a road or pipeline has been constructed and maintained adequately or poorly.

A range of access, quality, and price variables cover different assessment measures of water, electricity, and telecommunications, including the percentage of households with access, hours of service or the percentage of calls dropped, and prices for connection and usage. To be comprehensive, price data should include official and unofficial payments—bribe payments for services can and should be tracked. In health and education, the World Bank's Service Delivery Indicators, which track measures such as presence at work, diagnostic accuracy, and adherence to clinical guidelines for doctors, drug availability and infrastructure quality at hospitals, knowledge of the syllabus and time taken instructing students for teachers, and textbook availability for schools, provide useful output indicators to match with health and learning outcomes.[29]

Regarding procurement, a system that uses competitive bids and pays out on the basis of outcomes avoids the trap of Gresham's law—that bad money drives out good money. Bad bidders cannot win on the basis of low price through skimping on delivery because they are not paid until the goods or services are delivered and evaluated. Focusing on outcomes is simply the only way to ensure that competition delivers results, and it is the best way to reduce the threat of corruption diminishing the impact of spending. Output- and performance-based road contracts are one example in transport: they involve payments, often made monthly, for road maintenance (and now increasingly for construction) based on the number of kilometers of road maintained to a certain standard over a given period of time. Indicators of maintenance include road availability, the speed obtainable, and other parameters that can be monitored easily, even by the public. Although such output-based contracts cannot entirely preclude all acts of corruption, they are awarded using competitive processes based on the lowest required payment for achieving the stipulated outputs, and payments are made only after the outputs are delivered. Contracting out, combined with a focus on results, can help to improve the delivery of education services as well.

Of course, an approach that focuses on governance inputs (competition, simplification, and transparency) and sector outcomes (service coverage, learning outcomes, mortality) will commit sins of both omission and commission regarding corruption. In terms of empirical analysis, studies may suggest that a governance intervention like tracking when teachers and doctors deliver learning or health leads to improved outcomes, but it would be a false positive to ascribe this improvement to reduced corruption because the impact was through some other channel (such as improved knowledge or decreased incompetence). Studies also may suggest that a governance intervention fails to improve outcomes, but it would be a false negative to suggest it had not reduced corruption, because corruption did fall, but this impact was offset by some other factor—corruption was replaced by legal lobbying that as effectively reduced returns to utility investment, for example.

---

29 The World Bank's Service Delivery Indicators are available at http://datatopics.world bank.org/sdi/.

These false positives or negatives may be a problem for those concerned with the morality of bureaucrats as judged by the legal status of their corrupt actions. Yet it is not clear what approaches would work more reliably to uncover the corruption that is not uncovered by a focus on outputs. Furthermore, a governance intervention that improves outcomes is to be welcomed regardless of the causal chain through which it accomplishes that feat. Conversely, an intervention that somewhat reduces illegal payoffs but does so, for instance, at the cost of dramatically lowering vaccine coverage is not a successful intervention. Interventions that increase corruption while improving outcomes are likely to be rare and should be of even less concern.

Many activities that governments undertake—and should undertake—are not related to outcomes that are widely agreed upon or easily measureable. In education, for example, not only is the measurement of learning a conflicted and complex field, but schooling is also about a range of other outcomes including socialization, child care, and employment, some of which are hard to measure and can only be judged subjectively, one against another. This challenge becomes more acute across sectors, where approaches like cost-benefit analysis are partial and unsatisfactory solutions.[30] From the standpoint of minimizing corruption risk as much as from that of overall contracting efficiency, the best approach is one that should be applied regardless of that corruption, such as by contracting out services at the level where contracts (and accompanying laws and regulations) can best specify all of the outcomes desired from the assignment. This is the standard concern with contractual completeness, involving outcomes or outputs rather than inputs.[31] In some cases it may be at the level of the individual, in others at the level of multiple local firms, and in yet others at the level of a single national contract. Once again, this approach is at best a partial answer: for many services that governments should provide, there is no level at which contracting can be (transparently) complete. But it is still valuable to make the effort to design contracting to work at the level where contract performance can best be judged.

---

30 Frank (2000).
31 Domberger and Jensen (1997).

Conclusion

Governments should reduce the coercive reach of the state by limiting regulations and government ownership of firms to where they are most necessary. Doing so would allow governments to focus their capacity on measuring and publishing data on inputs, outputs, and outcomes in order to improve service delivery and reduce corruption. Such indicators could include bribe payments for service delivery and levels of absenteeism as but two of many quality metrics. That monitoring has to be done by governments; perhaps the biggest role for donors is to support such efforts.

5

Practical Policymaking for Donors

A caricature of how donors' practices have changed in reaction to corruption and weak governance over the past quarter-century would be as follows: members of the aid industry looked at how their investment projects were performing and found the results wanting. They concluded that policies and institutions were the problem. So they kept doing investment projects with a bit more in the way of procurement and financial management oversight, but really focused on the policy dimensions: training, technical assistance for privatization and corruption watchdogs, and the like.

Corrupt clients were happy because technical assistance is particularly difficult to monitor and per diems for attending training are always nice. Noncorrupt clients were sometimes happy because, once in a while, lack of technical expertise really was the major obstacle to reform and donor countries actually had some expertise that translated well to different country settings—but that was an exception. Most clients simply did not care.

But one result of this focus on policy over performance was that aid agencies retired their engineers and technical experts and left projects in the hands of policy experts, auditors, and economists who had no experience in judging the quality of an investment project. And so now the technical assistance advice is regularly ignored and investment project oversight focuses increasingly on inputs, not outputs. This has created a huge missed opportunity: the response to concerns about aid outcomes should have been to pay more attention to monitoring those outcomes, not less.

Making the problem worse is that beyond evaluators' limited ability to measure corruption and limited knowledge of how to reduce it or ring-fence investment projects from it, there are limits to how much donors can deal with the type of corruption that is the real concern of people in developing and rich countries alike. As Daron Acemoglu and James Robinson have suggested, "corruption is a symptom, not the disease. . . . But Western politicians, multinationals and international organizations are . . . drawn to the idea of fighting corruption because the existing rules of international engagement place the political roots of these problems off-limits."[1] This constraint leads, for example, to an embarrassed silence over human rights abuses while storms of complaint rage over incomplete bid documents.

In short, regardless of the model used in aid-funded investment projects, and especially given the limited ability of donors to tackle the underlying issues at the heart of popular concerns over corruption, the role of foreign aid in improving governance and corruption is likely to be limited. The donors are bit-players, using equipment that does not work very well. But despite these issues, there is still a considerable agenda for donors in the anticorruption space.

Does Ring-Fencing Work?

If corruption is a cancer, the chemotherapy of ring fencing—special procurement rules and financial procedures with heavy donor oversight—may in some cases be worse than the disease. As important, there is limited evidence that it kills the cancer cells. In fact, there is no good evidence on the efficacy of the suite of donor-imposed financial and procurement oversight on levels of corruption, even though both donors and recipients spend much time and effort attempting to manage it.

With regard to procurement procedures, the procurement process is about more than merely corruption: it is designed to maximize real competition and achieve value for money. Some standard procurement rules have made a real difference in that regard: greater advertising under World Bank

---

1 Acemoglu and Robinson (2015).

procurement rules, for example, leads to more competition, which in turn leads to lower prices.[2] That said, many of the details of the prescribed procurement process are justified on the grounds that they reduce opportunities for malfeasance, but there is limited evidence of their efficacy. For example, there has been no survey comparing reported bribes for donor-funded contracts to bribes for similar contracts funded by recipient governments. Available evidence suggests that ring-fencing does not work very well: a recent survey of firms that bid on international contracts found that only 15 percent of respondents thought that tender rules were an obstacle to corruption.[3]

Even without good evidence on the efficacy of procurement and fiduciary oversight on controlling corruption in projects, it is clear that, for all the disruption in country relations and program implementation they can cause, corruption investigations rarely turn up major corruption in aid. An analysis of cases brought to the World Bank's Evaluation and Suspension Office between 2007 and 2012 found cases of fraud or corruption that led to sanctions in 157 contracts worth $245 million. But only 30 percent of those contracts involved corruption; the rest involved fraud. This suggests around $75 million worth of contracts over that time were found to involve corruption. Considering that the World Bank lending portfolio is a thousand times as large, corruption is either effectively a nonissue in World Bank contracting or the bank's investigations are not finding and proving it to any great effect.[4]

Evidence of the benefits of ring-fencing and investigation is largely missing, yet there are considerable costs associated with donor procurement oversight and methods. A recent sampling of 120 World Bank–financed client-executed consulting procurements found that the average selection process took 17 months in total—equivalent to 64 percent of the average contract duration—including 131 days between proposal submis-

---

2 See Kenny and Crisman (2016).

3 Søreide (2006). There is some evidence that World Bank–financed procurements are sometimes being won by firms with the greatest comparative advantage in bribery rather than leading global firms that can deliver the best product at the lowest price (Kenny and Musatova 2012).

4 Alexander and Fletcher (2012). Related to this, Søreide, Gröning, and Wandall (2016, p. 546) note that "there has not been a single study seeking to determine whether sanctions are associated with greater integrity, fairness, and competition in markets or with a noticeable reduction in corruption and fraud."

sion and transmission of evaluation reports to the World Bank.[5] What is more, procurement delays do not seem to relate to the income level of the countries, suggesting it is the procurement system that produces bad results, not client capacity.[6]

The bidding process for goods and works under World Bank–financed contracts fares little better. A review of infrastructure contracts finds low bidding rates, low foreign participation, minimal participation of world-leading firms, and 200-day-plus finalization times for large contracts.[7] Again, country capacity cannot explain these outcomes; they appear to be systemic issues.

Furthermore, donor procurement oversight and financial management systems alone can never be enough to ensure quality delivery. As mentioned earlier, lowest-price competition that does not monitor outcomes can be positively harmful: good contractors bid a reasonable price while bad contractors can bid low prices at which the work cannot be completed to standard.[8] Such firms can get away with delivering poor quality if no one monitors the outcomes, and poor-quality work can incur a far higher economic cost than bribes that raise bid prices. When the donor response to corruption concerns is to hire more procurement and financial management specialists rather than more experts who can judge the quality of investments made, they simply exacerbate this problem. And this has been an all-too-standard response. When the World Bank discovered fraud and collusion associated with poor delivery of contracted goods and services in Indian health projects, it hired the United Nations Office for Project Services as a procurement agent, three people to advise on governance issues, three others as additional procurement staff, and just one sector expert to support monitoring and evaluation: a six-to-one ratio of procurement and governance hires to hires with actual sector expertise.[9]

---

5 Casartelli and Wolfstetter (2007).

6 Bidding costs to firms were considerable: the median value of a contracting assignment procured using the quality- and cost-based selection method was $432,000. Proposal preparation for short-listed firms can cost between $30,000 and $60,000. Given an average short list of five, this suggests total preparation costs of between 35 and 70 percent of final contract values.

7 Kenny and Musatova (2012).

8 Manelli and Vincent (1995).

9 World Bank, February 28, 2008, "India – Detailed Implementation Review," http://on line.wsj.com/public/resources/documents/IndiaDIRBankResponse.pdf.

The problems with baroque oversight of developing-country procurements and project management by donors, however, are small compared to the most common alternative, which is to simply channel aid through firms and civil society organizations based in donor countries. The 2005 Paris Declaration on Aid Effectiveness, a consensus set of donor best practices in aid delivery, highlights the importance of aligning aid with the priorities of recipient countries through such measures as using recipient countries' public financial management systems and procurement systems, avoiding parallel project implementation units, making aid predictable and untying it from sourcing requirements that benefit the donor country, and coordinating technical assistance with national development strategies. The more aid is channeled around rather than through recipient governments, the less any of these beneficial measures are likely to happen.

The Global Partnership for Effective Development Cooperation, a multistakeholder group monitoring the rollout of aid effectiveness principles, tracks "disbursements for the government sector" for a sample of aid recipients. This is "development co-operation funding disbursed in the context of an agreement with administrations (ministries, departments, agencies or municipalities) authorized to receive revenue or undertake expenditures on behalf of central government. This includes works, goods or services delegated or subcontracted by these administrations to other entities."[10] The group also tracks how much of that funding is executed through recipient countries' budgets and how much uses their auditing, procurement, and financial reporting systems.[11] Those percentages are small. Only 16 to 34 percent of aid uses recipient countries' procurement systems. For U.S. aid, 12 to 46 percent is disbursed with government-agency agreement, and just 2 to 6 percent uses recipient countries' procurement systems. (The Global Partnership process only tracks approximately half of the aid that donors report having delivered to the sample of recipient countries, so it is possible to report only an approximate range for outcomes on these measures.) Table 5-1 shows results for other countries and multilateral donors. The considerable majority of bilateral aid is delivered

---

10 Global Partnership for Effective Development Co-operation (2013, p. 28).
11 OECD, April 3, 2014, "Making Development Co-operation More Effective," www.oecd
   -ilibrary.org/development/making-development-co-operation-more-effective_
   9789264209305-en.

Table 5-1. Donors Are Not Following Paris Recommendations (in US$ millions)

Donor	Country programmable aid (2012)	Total disbursements reported (2013)	Disbursements for government sector . . .	. . . using country procurement systems
European Union	7,296	2,874	2,158	896
France	4,851	778	655	584
Germany	4,255	1,510	1,341	670
Japan	11,786	4,527	4,425	3,098
Norway	1,116	420	235	125
United Kingdom	4,419	1,651	973	530
United States	14,635	3,655	1,687	236
World Bank	9,706	8,699	8,673	3,152
African Development Bank	1,693	1,559	1,465	608
Asian Development Bank	1,823	2,509	2,505	1,289
TOTAL	88,158	40,898	33,514	13,973

using a mechanism that the international community considers ineffective, and ring-fencing is one big reason (or excuse) for why this happens.

Regardless of its costs and efficacy in deterring procurement corruption, ring-fencing fences in only a small part of what matters to outcomes. The evidence from a large sample of World Bank–funded projects is that, in general, the bigger challenge to achieving results in investment lending is not procurement risk, but delivery risk. World Bank economists Gerhard Pohl and Dubravko Mihaljek find that factors such as cost overruns and delays in delivery are comparatively minor in determining the gap between economic rates of return on World Bank projects estimated during project design and reestimated after the project was completed. Factors before and after the procurement process made the largest difference.[12]

This is because governance failures can significantly reduce the macroeconomic impact of a project even if the project itself is carefully chosen, well-designed and built, and free from corruption.[13] Not least, other projects that are part of the government's investment plans rejected for donor financing may be funded domestically instead, so that the overall quality of the recipient's capital stock is unaffected by oversight of the donor-selected project. Or operation and maintenance budgets may be too low to sustain existing stocks of infrastructure, as reflected in poor indicators of quality in many countries. A project-based approach to corruption misses these impacts, which frequently are at the core of the overall development impact of failed governance.[14]

Not only does ring-fencing affect only a few of the factors that determine whether a project will succeed, it also usually involves a tiny part of recipient countries' budgets. Government spending in developing countries is now $5.9 trillion a year, while official development assistance (ODA) from members of the Development Assistance Committee of the OECD totals $0.15 trillion. On average, ODA is worth around 7 percent of total international inflows and 2.5 percent of government spending in

---

12 Pohl and Mihaljek (1992).

13 For example, *Infrastructure at the Crossroads* (World Bank 2006) noted that World Bank staff, "in the context of the broader sector dialogue, spend a substantial amount of time steering government officials away from poorly designed projects." This is an important effort, but it may have a macro impact only if the effort is to stop such investments from occurring at all, rather than to stop them from occurring under Bank projects.

14 Kenny (2006).

recipient countries. In 1990, ODA was the largest international resource flow for 95 countries worldwide, but today that number has dropped to 43 countries with a combined population of 660 million people.[15] ODA amounts to more than 25 percent of government spending in just 19 of those remaining 43 countries, with a combined population of only 160 million. (Afghanistan, the Democratic Republic of the Congo, and Ethiopia account for more than 70 percent of that combined population.)[16]

Much aid provided directly to developing countries effectively finances a small percentage of the marginal investment projects on a government's wish list. Under those circumstances, ring-fencing should not have a huge impact on macro development outcomes in most countries, regardless of whether such defensive practices worked. And direct budget support makes far more sense. In countries where aid accounts for a very small part of investment, a (ring-fenced) project model makes sense only when there are strong reasons to think that investment patterns would look considerably different if the project did not exist.

The traditional project model should be used to test a new technology or approach, and in cases where fungibility of funds is less of an issue (that is, where it is needed to fund projects that would be unlikely to occur in the absence of aid). One example is delivering global or regional public goods at the local level; another is support of governance activities. Far more aid ought to flow to the provision of global public goods, innovative approaches, new technologies, and (potentially) governance, but for most aid recipients nearly all aid outside of those categories should take the form of budget support.

For the projects that still make sense, donors such as the World Bank could do a lot of good by randomly auditing, financially and physically, a small subset of processes and outcomes after the fact, rather than auditing all contract procurement processes and financial flows of all projects during their execution.[17] The red flags in traditional, targeted procurement audits appear to be weak indicators of actual problems,[18] so random audits may be only somewhat less effective at uncovering corruption than targeted audits. More important, these random, ex post facto audits would

---

15 Calculated from Development Initiatives (2013).

16 Ibid.

17 Savedoff (2016).

18 Kenny and Musatova (2012).

provide the basis for objective analysis of the level of financial and implementation mismanagement across a donor's portfolio, which cannot be
gleaned by targeted audit approaches. Random audits would provide a far
more useful measure of institutional weakness and aid effectiveness than
perception indicators or surveys of general bribe incidence, and they could
help evaluate the actual impact of ring-fencing and other approaches on
malfeasance. They also would allow for a lighter-touch set of rules and
procedures on other projects in the portfolio, reducing the harm that ring-
fencing does to delivering results.

Donors Should Focus on Outcomes and Outputs, Even More Than Recipient Governments

Donors should ensure that money reached its intended destinations and
recipients. If an investment project calls for local governments to procure
goods, it should be possible to track flows from the donor through the
central and local government to firms providing those goods. Programs
such as the International Aid Transparency Initiative, which produces
data on financial flows, are vital in that regard. Nonetheless, at the very
least, donors should significantly increase the proportion of monitoring
resources applied to ensuring that high-quality goods, works, and services
actually have been delivered in projects while reducing the proportion applied to procurement and fiduciary controls. Where possible, they should
move to payment on the basis of that delivery or—even better—the results
it is meant to achieve. If donors pay on the basis of transparent development outcomes, they provide the incentive for recipient governments to
find institutional reforms that deliver more for less, offering less space for
waste and malfeasance.

Cash-on-delivery approaches pay governments on the basis of development outcomes achieved, on a proportional basis, for example, for each
additional student who completes schooling and takes a test, or each additional 18-month-old who receives a full course of vaccines and immu-
nizations. The payments are based on a survey of progress and can be set
lower than the cost of provision to ensure that governments themselves
have to provide financing and thereby show their commitment to the outcomes as well. The model obviates the need for the procurement and fiduciary controls of current project models and allows governments to adapt

and evolve approaches that work in their localities rather than be stuck with a program designed in a distant donor capital. The UK Department for International Development is financing such an approach in Ethiopia with education. It is a model that can work, and perhaps would work even better, in most fragile states.

Where donors are acting as the safety net of last resort, providing health care or basic education, they can use output-based payments to remunerate the providers guaranteeing the access to and quality of the services. Take the case of the successful Afghanistan health program so disliked by the U.S. Special Inspector General for Afghanistan Reconstruction because the financial management system in the Afghan Ministry of Health was not up to scratch. Under results-based payments, financing would not stop because harried officials failed to perfectly follow every paragraph of a 100-page procurement manual. As long as children were vaccinated and women had access to family planning, the ministry would receive $4.50 per person covered. Or, to put it more simply, if the program delivers impressive results at an incredibly low price, the ministry gets paid.

Furthermore, results payments can be combined with conditional cash transfers to poor people themselves. Randomized evaluations of programs that pay students for attending schools and parents for ensuring that their children get basic health care suggest that such payments can have considerable returns.[19] Comparatively simple survey methods work to track development outcomes in these cases, suggesting less need for active direct engagement in the "procurement process" of cash handouts.[20]

Much of what governments can and should do is not easily or uncontroversially measured. Similarly, paying for results is not always simple or uncontroversial. Budget or humanitarian support to governments that are systematic abusers of human rights, for example, does not fit with the model. But it is exactly where results are very difficult to measure that the potential for diversion is at its greatest. Imagine a donor financing a government to hire a consultant to provide confidential advice on transactions that will themselves remain confidential (such as for gas exploration agreements). The donor may force the recipient government to produce evidence of a procurement process and financial transfers, but it will have no way of truly knowing if the consultant has pocketed the money (minus

---

19 Diepeveen and van Stolk (2012).
20 Haushofer and Shapiro (2016).

a bribe or two) and provided no advice. If donors cannot measure results, they cannot guarantee that aid has been used with probity and effect.

Outcome-based aid also is not simple for projects that take time to show success or failure. In education projects, for example, test outcomes could take years to respond to new educational initiatives. Recipients may not be willing to wait that long for payments, and donors may be uncomfortable with the complexities of budgeting for potential expenditures that far in the future. To accommodate longer time frames, such projects could have a sliding scale of financing from contracting on an input basis toward an output basis (higher teacher attendance) or outcome basis (test scores). Similarly, there could be a sliding scale for the focus of monitoring from process measurement around inputs to output and outcome measurement. The point is to move aid projects as far as possible along each scale. Moving financing toward projects that can be linked to measurable outcomes or outputs, even if full results-based financing is impossible, is a powerful anticorruption procedure.

And donors have this choice. They do not have to fund everything that governments should do, so they can choose to fund the activities with results that are easier to monitor. Some of those areas are where there is the best evidence that aid works, such as global health and cash transfers. By focusing on activities that can be measured, donors can both reduce the risk of corruption and demonstrate to taxpayers at home that aid finance is having a real impact.

Do Not Assume That Technical Assistance Is the Answer

Regarding technical assistance for governance and anticorruption, any number of World Bank evaluations have suggested that donors seldom are able to perceive what combination of formal institutional reforms will combine with existing formal and informal structures to deliver better development outcomes. Some such evaluations have concluded: "Within just a few years, the Bank has developed and mobilized a variety of tools . . . that bring the quality of public sector institutions into the spotlight. So far there is little evidence that governance is improving."[21] Others have voiced

---

21 World Bank (2004a). The World Bank's Operations Evaluation Department (OED) also suggests regarding programs that promote empowerment "both the intended and

similar concerns: "The Bank does not apply the same rigorous business practices to its capacity building work that it applies in other areas. Its tools . . . are not effectively used . . . [and] most activities lack standard quality assurance processes."[22]

More broadly, Harvard's Matt Andrews looked at 145 countries that introduced institutional reforms with donor agency support between 1998 and 2008. The Worldwide Governance Indicator for government effectiveness improved in about half the countries and worsened in about half.[23] Of course, the WGI indicator for government effectiveness may well not be capturing real change, but once again either the existing measures of governance are weak or donors' abilities to do anything about governance are weak—if not both.[24] Looking at outcomes rather than governance measures, Alina Rocha Menocal and Bhavna Sharma from the Overseas Development Institute analyzed 90 donor-backed citizen-voice and accountability interventions and found no evidence that the interventions had an impact on those outcomes. [25]

Evaluating anticorruption in particular, Tina Søreide from the Norwegian School of Economics concludes her review of the drivers of corruption by noting "the knowledge base is limited and diverse . . . [and] it is difficult for outsiders to steer administrative processes in a direction of what outsiders perceive conducive to fighting corruption. . . . Despite the huge amount spent on this agenda over the past two decades, up to now we have hardly any donor-financed methodologically robust impact evaluation results in anticorruption."[26] Given how little is known about what works at the country level to reduce corruption, it should come as little surprise that even less is known about how donors can help reduce it.

One reason for the gaps among technical assistance, institutional conditionality, and meaningful change involves a recipient response of "iso-

---

actual poverty impact of this type of intervention remain to be demonstrated" (p. xiv).

22 World Bank (2005). See also World Bank (2004b) on investment climate work: "World Bank Group strategies for improving the IC [investment climate] have suffered from a lack of knowledge about what types of institutional arrangements will work. . . . The feasibility of reform depends on the political economy of the reform process." See also Buch, Buntaine, and Parks (2015).

23 Andrews (2013, pp. 14–15).

24 Ibid.

25 Menocal and Sharma (2008).

26 Søreide (2014).

morphic mimicry" or "good governance facades."[27] These facades are bodies that have the outward appearance of an efficient bureaucratic institution but conceal dysfunction and corruption. Matt Andrews and Lant Pritchett from the Harvard Kennedy School and Michael Woolcock from the World Bank point to regulatory reforms designed to boost World Bank Doing Business scores but which have no impact on actual practices of regulatory discrimination as examples; Karl Moene from the University of Oslo and Tina Søreide point to anticorruption agencies for other case studies. Input measures of reforms taken would suggest programs that lead to governance facades are successful. The output of reduced corruption is hard to measure. Only a focus on development outcomes would allow a real assessment of success.

Another reason for the limited knowledge base beyond weak metrics for judging success is the likelihood that what works is context specific— that so-called best practices depend on existing cultural and institutional arrangements. This consideration has led to calls to "work with the grain" of local governance structures and let countries take the lead on the design of programs.[28] Such approaches may prove more successful, but there is not yet the evidence base to link them to better development outcomes.

Do Not Use Corruption Indicators to Direct Financing or Corruption Cases to Cut Flows

The use of governance and corruption indicators—or disclosed incidents of corruption—to determine aid flows has little empirical basis.[29] If aid is to be allocated on the basis of something other than poverty and the absence of public goods, it should be on empirical evidence of what it can achieve in a given setting. In this light, countries and sectors where improved outcomes can be most closely linked to increased aid flows should receive more aid.[30]

---

27 Andrews, Pritchett, and Woolcock (2013); and Moene and Søreide (2015).

28 Levy (2014).

29 Knack (2012) finds that perceptions of corruption determine donor willingness to implement Paris Declaration goals on use of country systems, as well as aid flows.

30 The U.S. Millennium Challenge Corporation explicitly uses multiple WGI indicators to measure distinct components of *ruling justly* and *encouraging economic freedom*. There is little evidence that this is empirically justifiable.

One predominant belief that has only weak empirical underpinning is that control of corruption, as measured by the WGI, is a larger, more foundational hurdle to broad-based development or aid effectiveness than ill health, poor education, low social capital, or other measures of institutional quality. In their study finding that overall measures of country policy and institutional strength correlate with improved outcomes from World Bank projects, Cevdet Denizer and Aart Kraay of the World Bank and Daniel Kaufmann of the Natural Resource Governance Institute also find that nearly four-fifths of the variation on outcomes is within countries, not across them. They suggest that their measure of the quality of the World Bank project manager is as important as all country-level factors combined in determining project outcomes.[31] To emphasize: corruption can derail and has repeatedly derailed aid projects. But a single national perceptions-based indicator of corruption is a very weak measure of the corruption risk, let alone the overall risk, that an aid project faces in any given country.

From this finding, a "hard hurdle" that denies aid flows to countries that rank poorly on corruption perceptions (as instituted by the U.S. Millennium Challenge Corporation [MCC]) seems to be particularly misguided. The idea of the hurdle is twofold: to incentivize and reward reform and to increase the effectiveness of MCC support. The MCC scorecard takes a fuzzy indicator and puts a bright, shining line down on top of it. Countries will not receive MCC support if they are in the bottom half of their income group on the control of corruption. This hurdle is a weak incentive to reform because it is difficult to know what policy levers move the control of corruption needle, and it is a weak tool for aid effectiveness because a fuzzy corruption indicator is (unsurprisingly) weakly related to development outcomes.

Conditionality around more reliable corruption measures would be preferable because it is less capricious: reported petty bribe payments or teacher or doctor absence, for example, are at least somewhat more concrete and actionable. However, these indicators would still suffer from the problem that they may not measure the corruption that matters to aid

---

31 Denizer, Kaufmann, and Kraay (2011). Once again, examination of World Bank project performance confirms the importance of "good countries" to project outcomes as measured by the bank's Independent Evaluation Group, but also suggests that big, complex projects run by inexperienced task managers fail more frequently. Still, it is also worth noting that all of these factors together explain approximately 12 percent of the variation in outcomes.

project outcomes. The empirical evidence in favor of any existing aid allocation mechanism around institutional factors is weak and detracts from a focus on reaching the poorest. The focus on fighting corruption using weak indicators may lead to policies that significantly reduce the overall impact of aid flows on development.

On a related note, the concept of zero tolerance has considerable appeal as a marketing phrase but turns out to be unimplementable in practice—a fact that many donor strategies implicitly or explicitly acknowledge. Take the Asian Development Bank's 1998 anticorruption strategy, which affirms "the importance of a 'zero tolerance' policy" but then notes that "different types of corruption will require different responses. There is a need for careful judgement."[32] The meaning of "zero tolerance" often is left intentionally unclear in donor discussions because it is not politically acceptable to say that some amount or types of corruption are tolerable. At the same time, some corruption inevitably will be associated with any effort to provide assistance in weakly governed countries. Furthermore, a zero tolerance approach that does not specify what the zero tolerance is for is counterproductive in an environment where corruption-prevention measures involve risk management. What tradeoffs in controls and design are acceptable in order to reduce the risk of corruption? Zero tolerance policies also encourage those involved in aid delivery to hide any evidence of potential corruption as deep as possible to avoid recriminations.

In reality, the only zero tolerance approach that is somewhat plausible is for bribery that is uncovered during project implementation and that directly involves donor funds. In these cases, donors can and should demand that recipient governments repay the misappropriated funds. But this hard approach cannot address the kind of corruption that prevents a project from reaching its intended result. Donors know that in some of the hospitals they have built, doctors will be taking side payments to prescribe and provide drugs, and that in the schools they build, some teachers will not turn up to teach when they are paid to do so, but such problems are ignored in the focus on receipts over results. Zero tolerance, in practice, also effectively ignores the many forms of corruption that a financial audit cannot easily capture. It focuses on a slogan over any sane idea of what aid is for or the damage that corruption might do.

---

32 Quoted in de Simone and Taxell (2014, p. 2).

Given the very few cases where aid has actually been stopped as a result of corruption, either such corruption is extremely rare or zero tolerance is a capriciously applied policy. One rare example: Germany suspended payments to the Global Fund in 2011 after the Global Fund inspector general unearthed corruption amounting to $34 million, or 0.3 percent of the organization's funds disbursed.[33] The donor cut off funds to an organization that had just demonstrated that it was trying to root out corruption, potentially sending the signal to other agencies to bury evidence of corruption. But even though the World Bank has uncovered corruption in a few of its projects, Germany has not cut off funding to the Bank's International Development Association, which makes low-interest loans to poor countries. Even zero tolerance for discovered bribery utilizing donor funds can be a difficult standard for donors to reach for political reasons. In another example, despite evidence of widespread corruption in a Norwegian aid project in Tanzania between 1994 and 2006, and even though Tanzania refunded hardly any of the misappropriated financing, Norway's aid program to Tanzania continued largely unabated.[34]

It is probably a good thing that, even in this narrow sense, zero tolerance often is abandoned. Punishing the Global Fund for uncovering corruption or cutting off aid to Tanzania because of corruption in one $60 million Norwegian project could easily overstep the bounds of fairness, proportionality, and efficiency considerations. More broadly, if donors really believe that corruption linked to 0.3 percent of funding is sufficient to cut off that funding while they continue to disburse ever-larger quantities of aid finance through a growing number of organizations, they also believe that corruption is not so much a common cancer but is more like a rare pimple.

Zero tolerance may seem a politically necessary slogan, but if it is to be effective then donors should develop and adhere to practical rules covering the question of how zero tolerance will be applied—be that as it may, aid funds will not be allocated to a recipient agency that continues to employ staff who have acted corruptly in the use of donor funds in the recent past. Otherwise, the slogan will continue to have a chilling effect on donor agency staff alongside ever-decreasing credibility with donor recipients and constituents.

---

33 Boseley (2011).
34 Jansen (2013).

What Should Donors Do Beyond a Focus on Outcomes?

Harking back to the two routes for development progress suggested in chapter 2—better governance and better outcomes at the same level of governance—there is a large role for aid in support of governance-related public goods, those that improve national governance (for example, supporting organizations such as local chapters of Transparency International) and those that coordinate global governance responses through the World Trade Organization and the United Nations (UN) Convention Against Corruption and the UN Commission on International Trade Law.

At the national level, there is also a role for donors in backing "positive deviants" including corruption hunters like Nuhu Ribadu and international efforts to return resources pilfered by corrupt leaders to the countries that rightfully own them—with the necessary caveat that the impact is likely to be marginal. According to an analysis sponsored by the Stolen Assets Recovery Initiative, only $147.2 million in stolen assets was returned by OECD members between 2010 and June 2012, and $276.3 million was returned between 2006 and 2009—"a fraction of the $20–40 billion estimated to have been stolen each year."[35] The report's upper end estimate suggests stolen assets equaled 0.35 percent of developing country GDP between 2006 and 2012, and asset recovery equaled 0.15 percent of stolen assets.[36]

Donors also have a key role to play in supporting the global public good of knowledge and information: lesson-sharing and knowledge generation through efforts like the U4 Anti-Corruption Resource Center, as well as the surveys of bribery levels and related institutional issues that provide the best available evidence on the extent and nature of corruption across the world. Donors also should back coalitions of the willing through institutions including the Extractive Industries Transparency Initiative, the Open Government Partnership, and Open Contracting Partnership, along with civil society organizations that report on corruption, often at considerable risk.

A small amount of financing can have a dramatic impact on outcomes, especially when donor governments themselves lead by example and support global collaborative learning. To take the example of the Open Con-

---

35 Gray and others (2014).

36 World Bank, n.d., "GDP at Market Prices (Constant 2010 US$)," http://data.world bank.org/indicator/NY.GDP.MKTP.KD?display=graph (accessed March 23, 2016).

tracting Partnership and its collaborators, including the Construction Sector Transparency Initiative and the Extractive Industries Transparency Initiative, this donor-supported group was able to build on the leadership of the British government in publishing government contracts and data to create a rapidly expanding global norm: in 2010, there were only two known cases of routine publication; by 2014, there were nine. At a 2016 anticorruption conference in London, 14 governments including Afghanistan, France, Georgia, Nigeria, the United Kingdom, and the United States announced that they would implement the Open Contracting Data Standard.[37] Perhaps donors in particular should back efforts to make aid flows considerably more transparent, such as the International Aid Transparency Initiative. Worryingly, data from Publish What You Fund suggest that the publication of results is often one of the weakest parts of donor transparency commitments and deliverables.[38]

Donors also have a part to play in reducing the need for strong institutions through technology. The mobile phone is one such technology discussed earlier, but so are its offshoots. The UK's DFID helped finance Vodafone's early experiments with mobile banking in Kenya, which evolved into the M-PESA banking platform as well as smart cards that allow for cash transfers to be made directly into the hands of poor people in the north of the country.[39] Both interventions have demonstrated the potential for mobile communications to massively expand financial services, including targeted transfers from governments at costs a fraction of earlier systems and with far less likelihood of leakage.

Other sectors provide different examples. Chapter 4 mentioned biometric technologies; the issue of medical diagnosis is another area with big potential for technological advance. One major factor behind high mortality in developing countries is misdiagnosis by doctors who ask as few as one question of their patients. Those who are lucky enough to actually receive treatment may be treated for diseases they do not have. World Bank research has suggested that three years of additional medical training im-

---

37 Charles Kenny, May 13, 2016, "Huge Progress on Open Contracting in London," www. cgdev.org/blog/huge-progress-open-contracting-london.

38 See, for example, USAID: Publish What You Fund, n.d., "U.S., USAID," http://tracker. publishwhatyoufund.org/publish/organisations/US-1/publication/.

39 Lisa Phillips, August 8, 2015, "Talking Technology with My Mum: DFID's Role in M-PESA," UK DFID, https://dfid.blog.gov.uk/2013/08/15/talking-technology-with-my-mum-dfids-role-in-m-pesa/.

proved diagnostic performance in Tanzania by just 1 percent. The return on technological advances can be much higher. Technology can empower patients with more knowledge about what ails them—in other words, it can create informed consumers. Cheap and simple diagnostic kits could allow patients to test for common diseases themselves. Diagnostics for All, a nonprofit medical firm, is working on a range of such simple tests that can be used in the developing world.[40] These tests employ paper-based kits that do not require clean water, syringes, refrigeration, equipment, or skilled technicians. The initial Diagnostics for All project is designed to spot the side effects of medicines used to treat people with tuberculosis and HIV/AIDS in developing countries. The test, targeted to cost 10 cents or less, will change color depending on liver toxicity levels. Cheap, reliable diagnostics for a range of diseases could help reduce poor people's reliance on doctors who are not delivering good-quality care.

There is a significant role for donor support across a range of development technologies. Promising examples include the agricultural research group CGIAR, which supports technology development to improve agricultural yields in developing countries; Global Development Innovation Ventures, which uses an evidence-based approach to support, test, and scale innovative solutions to development challenges; and organizations that develop and test small-scale energy-generation systems that might allow competitive energy provision in poor countries.

Finally, a number of domestic and multilateral activities beyond aid might help improve governance outcomes in developing countries. Donor countries should ensure that critical governance structures such as public registries of beneficial ownership (to reveal who controls firms and property), open contracting, and tax-information exchanges are put into place. They should support efforts to track financial flows, while trying to avoid the unintended consequences of the current, poorly designed money-laundering rules.[41] Evidence suggests, for example, that the OECD Anti-Bribery Convention has reduced how much rich-country firms engage with parts of the developing world that are perceived to be particularly corrupt. (Of course, this may be something of a pyrrhic victory from the

---

40　See the Diagnostics for All website at http://dfa.org/.

41　CGD Working Group Report, 2015, "Unintended Consequences of Anti-Money Laundering Policies for Poor Countries," www.cgdev.org/sites/default/files/CGD-WG-Report-Unintended-Consequences-AML-Policies-2015.pdf.

point of view of developing countries.)[42] Multinational agreements to improve at least the formal rules governing transparency, accountability, and reporting may also have some role to play, with the caveat that the distance between de jure and de facto can be considerable.

Is a New Strategy Politically Realistic?

The common response to a more realistic approach to governance and anticorruption in aid policies is that it is politically naïve. Agencies that do not appear to have a strong command-and-control system and a large investigative team chasing every dollar will be flayed by politicians looking for any excuse to cut budgets. This argument is not convincing. Popular perceptions of corruption in aid have increased alongside a greater focus on the issue by aid agencies. The evidence suggests that talking about corruption in aid reduces support from both skeptics and supporters.

But if the strategy is unsuccessful, why is it used? In part, this strategy reflects the underlying view, as discussed in the introduction, that citizens in donor countries regard developing countries as charity cases. Charitable giving is intertwined with judgment: the more fortunate need to help these people because of their failings. The thinking goes that poor people are poor and need help because they are lazy or ill educated, or their leaders are incompetent or corrupt. When recipients are seen as failed states on whom wealthier states bestow largesse, donors are less concerned about the lasting impact of their efforts because they have no expectations that their charity will have any effect. As long as the donation is delivered, donors can claim the moral satisfaction of suggesting that they have done what they could to help the less fortunate. This perspective easily leads donors to guarding their money against the recipients' failings by attach-

---

42 There is evidence that the 1977 Foreign Corrupt Practices Act had this impact on U.S. firms, with U.S. foreign direct investment diverted from countries perceived to be corrupt toward those perceived to be less so (Hines 1995). In countries where corruption is perceived to be widespread, this may leave construction or concession contracts to be bid on by a few local firms that face lower potential costs of corruption but may lack the capacity to carry out the work. Given the weak link between perceptions and levels of bribery, this suggests the potential for comparatively "clean" developing countries to suffer along the correctly targeted. A suboptimal response on the part of donors would be to further ring-fence projects to encourage international bidders (D'Souza 2012; and Sanyal and Samanta 2011).

ing lengthy conditions around who spends the money how and on what. It creates massive aid bureaucracies. It also creates the kind of aid system that has been so inefficient in delivering reconstruction in Haiti since the 2010 earthquake. This focus on the giving, rather than the impact, ensures that aid agencies spend far more time making sure that the money gets to where it is intended rather than making sure that the money achieves something when it is there. Donors are worried about countries "stealing from us" rather than us "shortchanging them."[43] The attention is on receipts, not results.

To improve effectiveness, aid appeals should be based not on the warm glow of moral superiority but rather on altruism, and there is at least some evidence that the strategy might work to grow aid budgets as well. Survey evidence suggests that 80 percent of Americans agree with the statement, "if I had more confidence that the aid we give to African countries would really help the people who need it I would be willing to increase the amount we spend on aid to Africa." By developing better ways to measure progress and focus aid for maximum results, donors could provide greater confidence that aid can really help.[44] The most effective way to head off the criticism that aid is being wasted is to point to its effectiveness in terms of actual results. The focus on outcomes—what did aid achieve in terms of children learning to read or being vaccinated—is a far stronger defense against aid fatigue than the hiring of another 20 procurement experts.[45]

Even though aid agencies may be able to drum up interest and donations in the short term by crying crisis at the hands of kleptocracy, in the longer term such a negative approach merely suggests the futility of all assistance that came before it. The resulting aid fatigue leads donor countries to despair at the prospect of "pouring money down foreign rat-holes," as former U.S. senator Jesse Helms put it.[46] It is far more sustainable to build support on a record of measured success. Donors are in a hole when it comes to the image of developing-country corruption. It is time for them to stop digging.

---

43 Thanks to Jonah Busch for this formulation.
44 Skelly, Chalisey, and Pierson (2010).
45 Marquette and others (2014).
46 "Obituary: Jesse Helms," July 6, 2008, *Independent* (London), www.independent. co.uk/news/obituaries/jesse-helms-powerful-republican-senator-who-championed-right-wing-causes-during-three-decades-in-861290.html.

Conclusion

For what it is worth, cross-country analyses using the WGI control of corruption measure find conflicting results, but recent analysis suggests that low levels of aid are associated with lower perceived corruption while higher levels of aid may see that relationship reverse.[47] This finding marginally adds to the concern that ring-fencing and technical assistance are having limited effect, especially in the most aid-dependent countries where donors might want to see the biggest impact for their expenditures. It further suggests the importance of nonaid approaches to reducing corruption.

Within the aid system itself, it is not clear that corruption is due to a lack of technical assistance for developing countries or that ring-fencing provides any meaningful protection to donor projects—or, for that matter, that ring-fencing provides relief from corruption that is worth the cost of the controls. Under the circumstances, a focus on outputs, outcomes, and results makes far more sense than relying on burdensome controls or unwanted advisory services to reduce the impact of corruption on development.

In short, while aid works,[48] it could work even better if it focused on delivering outcomes that national governments are unlikely to fund on their own—with or without taking corruption into account. But accounting for corruption, when aid does fund national investment priorities, it should do so as often as possible on the basis of a fair price for delivered results. This is the best method to ensure the rents that feed corruption are kept small.

---

47 Dalgaard and Olsson (2008).

48 For one recent contribution suggesting that aid can lead to economic growth, see Arndt, Jones, and Tarp (2015).

6
Reimagining the Development Dialogue

Any discussion of donors and corruption should take in some broader truths about the role of donor-funded projects in development. The aid project model was built in the 1950s under the assumption that the key constraint facing developing countries seeking rapid growth was lack of foreign exchange and domestic savings to fund investment. The model suggested that donors could fill these gaps and that the investment project process would ensure that external financing could be spent efficiently on investments that would generate high returns. That old justification no longer holds up. The investment-to-growth link is fragile: evidence shows the causal link from growth to levels of investment is stronger than the link from investment to growth.[1] Moreover, even if this justification for aid were to be used as the actual basis for funding allocation, aid flows are not large enough and do not follow the patterns expected for the model to be successful.[2]

It is also not true that development assistance is primarily about coun-

---

1 Kenny and Williams (2001).
2 Looking at aid as a source of foreign exchange, data from the 2008 World Development Indicators suggest that only 42 percent of aid flowed to countries where net development assistance was equal to or greater than one-third the value of international reserves. And countries do not appear to be using international flows to fund government investments that otherwise would not occur for lack of hard currency. In the period 2007–13, around 58 percent of the value of (preapproved) World Bank–financed con-

tries with successful institutions exporting those institutions to failing countries, using aid as a wedge. More often, development assistance is about helping countries that already are achieving broad-based development at historically unprecedented rates do so even faster, more efficiently, and more sustainably. Recognizing the secondary and supportive role of donors is vital to the quality of development assistance, the design of anti-corruption efforts, and efforts to create a stronger basis for future broad-based partnership between rich and poor countries.

These conclusions highlight some inconvenient truths for those who believe that the culture of corruption is a feature of poor countries and is a permanent and massive barrier to their development. Two points in particular stand out. First, if corruption is an immutable barrier to progress, and if macro measures of the pervasiveness of corruption suggest that its extent has remained mostly unchanged in spite of efforts to combat it, why has there been such massive and historically unprecedented progress in global development over the past two decades? Second, if bribery is the most insidious tool of those attempting to pervert the course of governance, why do the measures described in this book suggest that lobbying is more effective than bribery?

The truth about lobbying is that most people see it as corrupt, even if it is legal. It is time for the privileged elite of business leaders and international experts who are asked to rank countries on their perceived level of corruption to take note of this perception—and use a slightly less self-serving view of the corruption that they are evaluating. Furthermore, it is time for rich-world politicians to realize that they face exactly the same challenges that their colleagues in the developing world face: fighting corruption is about more than dollars under the table or enforcement of the law; it is about following the spirit of the laws and building trust among citizens that their voices really count.

There are other inconvenient truths for those in the aid industry who claim to understand corruption and how to respond to it. If a "culture of corruption" determines the outcomes of aid projects, then why is 80 percent of the variance of outcomes *within* countries, rather than *across* them? If corruption is so rampant and investigations into it have been successful, why is the corruption that those investigations have uncovered so limited?

---

tracts went to nationals of the borrowing country rather than foreign firms; see, for example. Kenny (2008).

Corruption is rarely the only or the overwhelming barrier to achieving results. As Bill Gates put it in a recent Gates Foundation letter, "[f]our of the past seven governors of Illinois have gone to prison for corruption, and to my knowledge no one has demanded that Illinois schools be shut down or its highways closed."[3] Corruption in Illinois—or India—might make government less efficient, but those governments still provide vital services. For that matter, donor countries frequently allow their aid to be used by people who do far worse things than divert some of it for personal gain. Governments that regularly torture or unjustifiably imprison their citizens, or deny the female half of their population rights they give to men, receive aid money. Military governments use donors' financial and material support—as well as tear gas—to suppress popular dissent.[4] Donor countries repeatedly have demonstrated positive tolerance for such activities.

Along with this inconsistency in enforcing standards of good governance, the cognitive inconsistency of supporting repressive governments suggests that donor countries' professed "zero tolerance" for corruption is more of a marketing ploy than a matter of principle. Perhaps the vaunted zero tolerance should focus more on gross human rights violations and children dying of diseases that can be prevented with a 20-cent vaccine rather than perceived levels of financial mismanagement.

But this book is not a call to care *less* about corruption. Donors should care, but they should care *better*. They should use approaches that are more likely to reduce corruption and its impact and less likely to have considerable unintended consequences in terms of delivering development. If official development assistance, and charitable giving, is to be used to support sustained development progress, it must focus on doing something useful rather than merely doing something. Looking more closely at outcomes is a tool to do that. When we use aid as a tool to leverage development, it is pointless to only demand a receipt: We should demand the result.

---

3 Gates (2014).
4 Morrison and Trew (2011); and Smith (2011).

References

Abouharb, Rodwan M., and Anessa L. Kimball. 2007. "A New Dataset on Infant Mortality Rates, 1816–2002." *Journal of Peace Research* 44: 743.

Abramo, Claudio Weber. 2008. "How Much Do Perceptions of Corruption Really Tell Us?" *Economics* 2, no. 3 (February), pp. 1–56.

Acemoglu, Daron, Simon Johnson, and James A. Robinson. 2001. "The Colonial Origins of Comparative Development: An Empirical Investigation." *American Economic Review* 91, no. 5 (December), pp. 1369–1401.

Acemoglu, Daron, and James Robinson. 2008. "The Role of Institutions in Growth and Development," Commission on Growth and Development Working Paper 10 (Washington, D.C.: World Bank).

———. 2015. "Corruption Is Just a Symptom, Not the Disease." *Wall Street Journal*. December 3.

Alatas, Vivi, and others. 2013. "Does Elite Capture Matter? Local Elites and Targeted Welfare Programs in Indonesia," Working Paper 18798 (Cambridge, Mass.: National Bureau of Economic Research).

Albouy, David Y. 2008. "The Colonial Origins of Comparative Development: An Investigation of the Settler Mortality Data," Working Paper 14130 (Cambridge, Mass.: National Bureau of Economic Research).

Alesina, Alberto F., Stelios Michalopoulos, and Elias Papaioannou. 2012. "Ethnic Inequality," Working Paper 18512 (Cambridge, Mass.: National Bureau of Economic Research).

Alexander, Myrna, and Charles Fletcher III. 2012. "Analysis of World Bank Completed Cases of Fraud and Corruption from the Perspective of Procurement." Background paper for *Review of the World Bank's Procurement Policies and Procedures* (Washington, D.C.: World Bank).

Andres, Luis, Jose Luis Guasch and Stephane Straub. 2007. "Do Regulation and Institutional Design Matter for Infrastructure Sector Performance?" (Washington, D.C: World Bank).

Andrews, Matt. 2013. *The Limits of Institutional Reform in Development: Changing Rules for Realistic Solutions* (Cambridge University Press).

Andrews, Matt, Lant Pritchett, and Michael Woolcock. 2013. "Escaping Capability Traps through Problem Driven Iterative Adaptation (PDIA)." *World Development* 51 (November), pp. 234–44.

Arndt, Channing, Sam Jones, and Finn Tarp. 2015. "Assessing Foreign Aid's Long-Run Contribution to Growth and Development." *World Development* 69 (May), pp. 6–18.

Ausland, Aaron, and Alfonso Tolmos. 2005. "Focus on Corruption: How to Secure the Aims of Decentralization in Peru by Improving Good Governance at the Regional Level." Mimeo (Cambridge, Mass: Kennedy School, Harvard University).

Bajari, Patrick, Robert McMillan, and Steven Tadelis. 2009. "Auctions versus Negotiations in Procurement: An Empirical Analysis." *Journal of Law, Economics, and Organization* 25, no. 2 (May), pp. 372–99.

Banerjee, Abhijit, and others. 2008. "Pitfalls of Participatory Programs: Evidence from a Randomized Evaluation in Education in India," Policy Research Working Paper 4584 (Washington, D.C.: World Bank).

Batra, Geeta, Daniel Kaufmann, and Andrew H. W. Stone. 2003. *Investment Climate around the World: Voices of the Firms from the World Business Environment Survey* (Washington, D.C.: World Bank).

Bazzi, Samuel, and Michael A. Clemens. 2013. "Blunt Instruments: Avoiding Common Pitfalls in Identifying the Causes of Economic Growth." *American Economic Journal: Macroeconomics* 5, no. 2 (April), pp. 152–86.

Beauchamp, Zack. 2016. "This Stunning Fact About Corruption in Brazil Helps Explain Its Political Crisis." Vox. April 18 (www.vox.com/2016/4/18/11450222/dilma-rousseff-impeachment-statistic).

Berg, Andrew G., and Jonathan D. Osrty. 2013. "Inequality and Unsustainable Growth: Two Sides of the Same Coin?" *International Organisations Research Journal* 8, no. 4, pp. 77–99.

Bertolini, Lorenzo. 2006. "How to Improve Regulatory Transparency: Emerging Lessons from an International Assessment," *Gridlines* no. 11 (Washington, D.C.: World Bank).

Birdsall, Nancy, Anna Diofasi, and Charles Kenny. Forthcoming. "What Drives Citizen Perceptions of Government Corruption? National Income, Petty Bribe Payments and the Unknown." CGD Working Paper (Washington, D.C.: Center for Global Development).

Bluhm, Richard, and Adam Szirmai. 2012. "Institutions and Long-Run Growth Performance. An Analytic Literature Review of the Institutional Determinants of Economic Growth," UNU-MERIT Working Paper Series, 2012—033 (IPD WP02) (Maastricht: United Nations University–Maastricht Economic and Social Research Institute on Innovation and Technology).

Boas, Taylor C., F. Daniel Hidalgo, and Neal P. Richardson. 2014. "The Spoils of Victory: Campaign Donations and Government Contracts in Brazil." *Journal of Politics* 76, no. 2 (April), pp. 415–29.

Bohlen, Celestine. 1999. "Earthquake in Turkey: Rage; Survivors Lead a Chorus of Demands to Punish the Builders." *New York Times*, August 20.

Boseley, Sarah. 2011. "Can the Global Fund Weather the Corruption Storm?" *Guardian* (London), January 28.

Bravo, David, Sankar Mukhopadhya, and Petra E. Todd. 2010. "Effects of School Reform on Education and Labor Market Performance: Evidence from Chile's Universal Voucher System." *Quantitative Economics* 1, no. 1 (July), pp. 47–95.

Brouthers, Lance E., Yan Gao, and Jason P. McNicol. 2008. "Corruption and Market Attractiveness Influences on Different Types of FDI." *Journal of Strategic Management* 29, no. 6 (June), pp. 673–80.

Buch, Benjamin P., Mark T. Buntaine, and Bradley C. Parks. 2015. "Aiming at the Wrong Targets: The Difficulty of Improving Domestic Institutions with International Aid," Working Paper 4 (Williamsburg, Va.: AidData, College of William and Mary).

Campos, Nauro F., Ralitza D. Dimova, and Ahmad Saleh. 2010. "Whither Corruption? A Quantitative Survey of the Literature on Corruption and Growth," IZA Discussion Paper 5334 (Bonn, Germany: Institute for the Study of Labor).

Campos, Nauro F., and Francesco Giovannoni. 2007. "Lobbying, Corruption and Political Influence." *Public Choice* 131, no. 1–2 (April), pp. 1–21.

Casartelli, Giovanni, and Elmar Wolfstetter. 2007. "World Bank Policy on the Selection and Employment of Consultants: Study of Its Effectiveness" (Washington, D.C.: World Bank).

Center for Global Development Working Group on Contract Publication. 2014. "Publishing Government Contracts: Addressing Concerns and Easing Implementation" (Washington D.C.: Center for Global Development).

Cheung, Yan Leung, P. Raghavendra Rau, and Aris Stouraitis. 2012. "How Much Do Firms Pay as Bribes and What Benefits Do They Get? Evidence from Corruption Cases Worldwide," Working Paper 17981 (Cambridge, Mass.: National Bureau of Economic Research).

Cingano, Federico. 2014. "Trends in Income Inequality and Its Impact on Economic Growth," OECD Social, Employment, and Migration Working Paper 163 (Paris: OECD Publishing).

Comin, Diego, William Easterly, and Erick Gong. 2010. "Was the Wealth of Nations Determined in 1000 BC?" *American Economic Journal: Macroeconomics* 2 (July), pp. 65–97.

Commander, Simon, and Zlatko Nikoloski. 2011. "Institutions and Economic Performance: What Can Be Explained?" *Review of Economics and Institutions* 2, no. 2 (Spring), pp. 1–35.

Corbacho, Ana, and others. 2016. "Corruption as a Self-Fulfilling Prophecy: Evidence from a Survey Experiment in Costa Rica." *American Journal of Political Science* 60, no. 4 (January), pp. 1077–92.

Crombrugghe, Denis de, and Kristine Farla. 2012. "Preliminary Conclusions on Institutions and Economic Performance," MERIT Working Paper 35 (Maastricht: United Nations University–Maastricht Economic and Social Research Institute on Innovation and Technology).

Dalgaard, Carl-Johan, and Ola Olsson. 2008. "Windfall Gains, Political Economy, and Economic Development." *Journal of African Economies* 17, sup. 1 (March), pp. 72–109.

Darnton, Andrew, and Martin Kirk. 2011. "Finding Frames: New Ways to Engage the UK Public in Global Poverty" (London: Bond for International Development).

Das, Binayak, and others. 2010. *Sharing the Reform Process: Learning from the Phnom Penh Water Supply Authority (PPWSA)* (Geneva: International Union for Conservation of Nature).

Davis, Jennifer. 2004. "Corruption in Public Service Delivery: Experience from South Asia's Water and Sanitation Sector." *World Development* 32, no. 1 (January), pp. 53–71.

DellaVigna, Stefano, and others. 2013. "Market-Based Lobbying: Evidence from Advertising Spending in Italy," Working Paper 19766 (Cambridge, Mass.: National Bureau of Economic Research).

Denizer, Cevdet, Daniel Kaufmann, and Aart Kraay. 2011. "Good Countries or Good Projects? Macro and Micro Correlates of World Bank Project Performance," Policy Research Working Paper 5646 (Washington, D.C.: World Bank).

Department of Justice, U.S. 2008. "Siemens AG and Three Subsidiaries Plead Guilty to Foreign Corrupt Practices Act Violations and Agree to Pay $450 Million in Combined Criminal Fines" (Washington, D.C., December 15).

Development Initiatives. 2013. "Investments to End Poverty" (Bristol, UK: Development Initiatives).

Diepeveen, Stephanie, and Christian van Stolk. 2012. "How Effective Are CCTs in Low-Income Settings? A Review Exploring Factors Impacting on Programme Outcomes in Honduras and Nicaragua." RAND Working Paper (Santa Monica, Calif.: RAND Corporation).

Di Tella, Rafael, and Ernesto Schargrodsky. 2003. "The Role of Wages and Auditing during a Crackdown on Corruption in the City of Buenos Aires." *Journal of Law and Economics* 46, no. 1 (April), pp. 269–292.

Djankov, Simeon, and others. 2000. "The Regulation of Entry," Working Paper 7892 (Cambridge, Mass.: National Bureau of Economic Research).

———. 2009. "Disclosure by Politicians," Working Paper 14703 (Cambridge, Mass.: National Bureau of Economic Research).

Domberger, Simon, and Paul Jensen. 1997. "Contracting Out by the Public Sector." *Oxford Review of Economic Policy* 13, no. 4, pp. 67–78.

Donchev, Dilyan, and Gergely Ujhelyi. 2014. "What Do Corruption Indices Measure?" *Economics & Politics* 26, no. 2 (July), pp. 309–31.

Doucouliagos, Hristos, and Martin Paldam. 2010. "Conditional Aid Effectiveness: A Meta-Study." *Journal of International Development* 22, no. 4 (April), pp. 391–410.

D'Souza, Anna. 2012. "The OECD Anti-Bribery Convention: Changing the Currents of Trade." *Journal of Development Economics*, 97, no. 1 (January), pp. 73–87.

Durlauf, Steven N., Andros Kourtellos, and Chih Ming Tan. 2008. "Are Any Growth Theories Robust?" *Economic Journal* 118, no. 527 (March), pp. 329–46.

Easterly, William, Jozef Ritzen, and Michael Woolcock. 2006. "Social Cohesion, Institutions, and Growth." *Economics & Politics* 18, no. 2 (July), pp. 103–20.

Eggers, Andrew, C., and Jens Hainmueller. 2013. "Capitol Losses: The Mediocre Performance of Congressional Stock Portfolios." *Journal of Politics* 75, no. 2 (April), pp. 535–51.

———. 2009. "MPs for Sale? Returns to Office in Postwar British Politics." *American Political Science Review* 103, no. 4 (November), pp. 513–33.

Ehrhardt, David, and others. 2007. "Economic Regulation of Urban Water and Sanitation Services: Some Practical Lessons," Water Sector Board Discussion Paper 9 (Washington, D.C.: World Bank).

Engerman, Stanley L., and Kenneth L. Sokoloff. 2002. "Factor Endowments, Inequality, and Paths of Development among New World Economics," Working Paper 9259 (Cambridge, Mass.: National Bureau of Economic Research).

Escresa, Laarni, and Lucio Picci. 2015. "A New Cross-National Measure of Corruption." *World Bank Economic Review* (July 24), pp. 1–31.

Estache, Antonio, Ana Goicoechea, and Lourdes Trujillo. 2006. "Utilities Reform and Corruption in Developing Countries." Mimeo (Washington, D.C.: World Bank).

Fay, Marianne, and Tito Yepes. 2003. "Investing in Infrastructure: What Is Needed from 2000 to 2010?" Policy Research Working Paper 3102 (Washington, D.C.: World Bank).

Ferraz, Claudio, and Frederico Finan. 2009. "Electoral Accountability and Corruption: Evidence from the Audits of Local Governments," Working Paper 14937 (Cambridge, Mass.: National Bureau of Economic Research).

Fisman, Raymond, Florian Schulz, and Vikrant Vig. 2012. "Private Returns to Public Office," Working Paper 18095 (Cambridge, Mass.: National Bureau of Economic Research).

Foltz, Jeremy D. and Kweku A. Opoku-Agyemang. "Do Higher Salaries Lower Petty Corruption? A Policy Experiment on West Africa's Highways." Working Paper (London: International Growth Centre).

Fowler, Wyche (U.S. Ambassador to Saudi Arabia). 1996. Diplomatic cable. WikiLeaks cable 96RIYADH4784, November 30 (https://wikileaks.org/plusd/cables/96RIYADH4784_a.html).

Frank, Robert H. 2000. "Why Is Cost-Benefit Analysis So Controversial?" *Journal of Legal Studies* 29, sup. 2 (June), pp. 913–30.

Galiani, Sebastian, and others. 2014. "The Effect of Aid on Growth: Evidence from a Quasi-Experiment," Policy Research Working Paper 6865 (Washington, D.C.: World Bank).

Gasmi, Farid, Paul Noumba Um, and Laura Recuero Virto. 2006. "Political Accountability and Regulatory Performance in Infrastructure Industries: An Empirical Analysis," Policy Research Working Paper 4101 (Washington, D.C.: World Bank).

Gassner, Katarina, Alexander Popov, and Nataliya Pushak. 2007. "An Empirical Assessment of Private Sector Participation in Electricity and Water Distribution in Developing Countries." Mimeo (Washington, D.C.: World Bank).

Gates, Bill. 2014. "Annual Letter 2014" (Seattle: Bill and Melinda Gates Foundation).

Gelb, Alan, and Julia Clark. 2013. "Identification for Development: The Biometrics Revolution," CGD Working Paper 315 (Washington, D.C.: Center for Global Development).

Glaeser, Edward L., and others. 2004. "Do Institutions Cause Growth?" *Journal of Economic Growth* 9, no. 3 (September), pp. 271–303.

Global Partnership for Effective Development Co-operation. 2013. "Guide to the Monitoring Framework of the Global Partnership" (New York).

Gray, Larissa, and others. 2014. *Few and Far: The Hard Facts on Stolen Asset Recovery* (Washington, D.C.: World Bank).

Gulati, Mohinder, and M. Y. Rao. 2006. "Checking Corruption in the Electricity Sector." Mimeo. (Washington, D.C.: World Bank).

Habib, Mohsin, and Leon Zurawicki. 2002. "Corruption and Foreign Direct Investment." *Journal of International Business Studies* 33, no. 2 (February), pp. 291–307.

Hallward-Driemeier, Mary, Gita Khun Jush, and Lant Pritchett. 2010. "Deals versus Rules: Policy Implementation Uncertainty and Why Firms Hate It," Policy Research Working Paper 5321 (Washington, D.C.: World Bank).

Hallward-Driemeier, Mary, and Lant Pritchett. 2011. "How Business Is Done and the 'Doing Business' Indicators: The Investment Climate When Firms Have Climate Control," Policy Research Working Paper 5563 (Washington, D.C.: World Bank).

Haushofer, Johannes, and Jeremy Shapiro. 2016. "The Short-Term Impact of Unconditional Cash Transfers to the Poor: Evidence from Kenya." *Quarterly Journal of Economics* 4, no. 131 (November), pp. 1973–2042.

Hellman, Joel S., and others. 2000. "Measuring Governance, Corruption, and State Capture: How Firms and Bureaucrats Shape the Business Environment in Transition Economies," Policy Research Working Paper 2312 (Washington, D.C.: World Bank).

Henderson, J. Vernon, and Ari Kuncoro. 2006. "Corruption in Indonesia," Working Paper 10674 (Cambridge, Mass.: National Bureau of Economic Research).

Hines, James R., Jr. 1995. "Forbidden Payment: Foreign Bribery and American Business after 1997," Working Paper 5266 (Cambridge, Mass.: National Bureau of Economic Research).

International Monetary Fund (IMF). 2016. "Corruption: Costs and Mitigating Strategies," IMF Staff Discussion Note SDN 16/05 (Washington, D.C.).

Jansen, Eirik G. 2013. "Don't Rock the Boat: Norway's Difficulties in Dealing with Corruption in Development Aid." In *Corruption, Grabbing and Development: Real World Challenges*, edited by Tina Søreide and Aled Williams (Bergen, Norway: Edward Elgar Publishing), pp. 186–95

Jie Bai, and others. 2013. "Does Economic Growth Reduce Corruption? Theory and Evidence from Vietnam," Working Paper 19483 (Cambridge, Mass: National Bureau of Economic Research).

Jinfeng Luo and Yi Wen. 2015. "Institutions Do Not Rule: Reassessing the Driving Forces of Economic Development," Paper FEDLWP2015-001 (St. Louis, Mo.: Federal Reserve Bank of St. Louis).

Johnsøn, Jesper, Nils Taxell, and Dominik Zaum. 2012. "Mapping Evidence Gaps in Anti-Corruption: Assessing the State of the Operationally Relevant Evidence on Donors' Actions and Approaches to Reducing Corruption." *U4 Brief* 2012, no. 7 (Bergen, Norway: Chr. Michelsen Institute).

Kaplan, David S., and Vikram Pathania. 2010. "What Influences Firms' Perceptions?" *Journal of Comparative Economics* 38, no. 4 (December), pp. 419–31.

Kapur, Devesh, and others. 2010. "Rethinking Inequality: Dalits in Uttar Pradesh in the Market Reform Era." *Economic and Political Weekly* 45, no. 35 (August 28 – September 3), pp. 39–49.

———. 2010. "The Worldwide Governance Indicators: Methodology and Analytical Issues," Policy Research Working Paper 5430 (Washington, D.C.: World Bank).

———. 2011. "The Worldwide Governance Indicators: Methodology and Analytical Issues." *Hague Journal on the Rule of Law*, 3, no. 2 (June), pp. 220–46.

Kennedy, Sam. 2010. "Nuhu Ribadu: Nigeria's Relentless Corruption Hunter." *PBS Frontline World*, January 28.

Kenny, Charles. 2005. "Why Are We Worried about Income? Nearly Everything That Matters Is Converging." *World Development* 33, no. 1 (January), pp. 1–19.

———. 2006. "Measuring and Reducing the Impact of Corruption in Infrastructure," Policy Research Working Paper 4099 (Washington, D.C.: World Bank).

———. 2007. "Infrastructure Governance and Corruption: Where Next?" Policy Research Working Paper 4331 (Washington, D.C.: World Bank).

———. 2008. "What Is Effective Aid? How Would Donors Allocate It?" *European Journal of Development Research* 20, no. 2 (June), pp. 330–46.

———. 2009. "Measuring Corruption in Infrastructure: Evidence from Transition and Developing Countries." *Journal of Development Studies* 45, no. 3 (February), pp. 314–32.

———. 2011. *Getting Better: Why Global Development Is Succeeding* (New York: Basic Books).

———. 2012. "Do We Still Need Development Goals?" (Washington, D.C.: Center for Global Development, February 16).

Kenny, Charles, and Ben Crisman. 2016. "Results Through Transparency: Does Publicity Lead to Better Procurement?" CGD Working Paper (Washington, D.C.: Center for Global Development).

Kenny, Charles, and Maria Musatova. 2012. "What Drives Contracting Outcomes in Infrastructure Procurement?" Mimeo (Washington, D.C.: World Bank).

Kenny, Charles, and William D. Savedoff. 2013. "Can Results-Based Payments Reduce Corruption?" Working Paper 345 (Washington, D.C.: Center for Global Development).

Kenny, Charles, and David Williams. 2001. "What Do Economists Know about Economic Growth—Or Why Don't They Know Very Much?" *World Development* 29, no. 1 (January), pp. 1–22.

Khan, Mushtaq. 2012. "Governance and Growth: History, Ideology and Methods of Proof." In *Good Growth and Governance in Africa: Rethinking Development Strategies*, edited by Akbar Noman, Kwesi Botchwey, Howard Stein, and Joseph Stiglitz (Oxford University Press), pp. 51–79.

Knack, Stephen. 2006. "Measuring Corruption in Eastern Europe and Central Asia: A Critique of the Cross-Country Indicators," Policy Research Working Paper 3968 (Washington, D.C: World Bank).

————. 2012. "When Do Donors Trust Recipient Country Systems?" Policy Research Working Paper 6019 (Washington, D.C: World Bank).

Kraay, Aart. 2015. "Weak Instruments in Growth Regressions: Implications for Recent Cross-Country Evidence on Inequality and Growth," Policy Research Working Paper 7494 (Washington, D.C: World Bank).

Kraay, Aart, and Peter Murrell. 2016. "Misunderestimating Corruption." *Review of Economics and Statistics* 98, no. 3 (July), pp. 455–66.

Langbein, Laura, and Stephen Knack. 2010. "The Worldwide Governance Indicators: Six, One, or None?" *Journal of Development Studies* 46, no. 2, pp. 350–70.

Levy, Brian. 2014. *Working with the Grain: Integrating Governance and Growth in Development Strategies* (Oxford University Press).

Lovei, Laszlo, and Dale Whittington. 1991. "Rent Seeking in Water Supply," Infrastructure and Urban Development Department Discussion Paper 1991 (Washington, D.C: World Bank).

Madani, Dorsati, and Martha Licetti. 2010. "Business Regulation, Reform, and Corruption," PREM Notes Economic Policy Number 155 (Washington, D.C: World Bank).

Magnier, Mark. 2010. "India Rocked by Mobile License Scandal." *Los Angeles Times*, December 9.

Manelli, Alejandro M., and Daniel R. Vincent. 1995. "Optimal Procurement Mechanisms." *Econometrica* 63, no. 3 (May), pp. 591–620.

Marquette, Heather, and others. 2014. "Communication in Anti-Corruption Work: Articulating Messages to Structure a Communication Plan." Background document for the Anti-Corruption Task Team of the OECD-DAC Governance Network (Paris: OECD).

Meagher, Patrick. 2002. *Anti-Corruption Agencies: A Review of Experience* (Washington, D.C.: World Bank).

Menocal, Alina Rocha, and Bhavna Sharma. 2008. *Joint Evaluation of Citizens' Voice and Accountability: Synthesis Report* (London: Overseas Development Institute).

Menocal, Alina Rocha, and others. 2015. "Why Corruption Matters: Understanding Causes, Effects and How to Address Them," DFID Evidence Paper on Corruption (London: UK Department for International Development).

Méon, Pierre-Guillaume, and Laurent Weill. 2008. "Is Corruption an Efficient Grease?" BOFIT Discussion Paper 20/2008 (Helsinki: Bank of Finland, Institute for Economies in Transition).

Milanovic, Branko. 2016. *Global Inequality: A New Approach for the Age of Globalization* (Harvard University Press).

Millennium Challenge Corporation. 2007. "Building Public Integrity through Positive Incentives: MCC's Role in the Fight against Corruption" (Washington, D.C.).

Minoiu, Camelia, and Sanjay G. Reddy. 2010. "Development Aid and Economic Growth: A Positive Long-Run Relation." *Quarterly Review of Economics and Finance* 50, no. 1 (February), pp. 27–39.

Moene, Kalle, and Tina Søreide. 2015. "Good Governance Facades." In *Greed, Corruption, and the Modern State: Essays in Political Economy*, edited by Susan Rose-Ackermand and Paul Lagunes (Northampton, Mass.: Edward Elgar Publishing), pp. 46–70.

Morrison, Sarah, and Bel Trew. 2011. "British-Made Tear Gas Was Used on Egypt's Protesters." *Independent* (London), December 3.

Muzzini, Elisa. 2006. "Consumer Participation in Infrastructure Regulation: Evidence from East Asia and Pacific Region," Working Paper 66 (Washington, D.C.: World Bank).

Natsios, Andrew. 2010. "The Clash of the Counter-Bureaucracy and Development," CGD Essay (Washington, D.C.: Center for Global Development).

OECD (Organization for Economic Cooperation and Development). 2013. "Aid for CSOs" (Paris: OECD, October).

Olken, Benjamin A. 2007. "Monitoring Corruption: Evidence from a Field Experiment in Indonesia." *Journal of Political Economy* 115, no. 2 (April), pp. 200–49.

———. 2009. "Corruption Perceptions vs. Corruption Reality." *Journal of Public Economics* 93, no. 7 (August), pp. 950–64.

Ostry, Jonathan David, and Andrew Berg. 2011. "Inequality and Unsustainable Growth: Two Sides of the Same Coin?" IMF Staff Discussion Note (Washington, D.C.: IMF).

Ostry, Jonathan David, Andrew Berg, and Charalambos G. Tsangarides. 2014. "Redistribution, Inequality, and Growth," IMF Staff Discussion Note (Washington, D.C.: IMF).

Paige, Jonathan. 2013. "British Public Wrong about Nearly Everything, Survey Shows." *Independent* (London), July 9.

Piketty, Thomas, and Emmanuel Saez. 2006. "How Progressive Is the US Federal Tax System? A Historical and International Perspective," Working Paper 12404 (Cambridge, Mass. National Bureau of Economic Research).

Pohl, Gerhard, and Dubravko Mihaljek. 1992. "Project Evaluation and Uncertainty in Practice: A Statistical Analysis of Rate-of-Return Divergences of 1,015 World Bank Projects." *World Bank Economic Review* 6, no. 2 (May), pp. 255–77.

Polgreen, Lydia, and Saimah Khwaja. 2010. "Delhi Building Collapse Tied to Bad Construction." *New York Times,* November 16.

Pritchett, Lant, Michael Woolcock, and Matthew Andrews. 2010. "Capability Traps? The Mechanisms of Persistent Implementation Failure," Working Paper 234 (Washington, D.C.: Center for Global Development).

Ramachandran, Vijaya, Ben Leo, and Ross Thuotte. 2011. *Supporting Private Business Growth in African Fragile States: A Guiding Framework for the World Bank Group in South Sudan, Somaliland, and Zimbabwe* (Washington, D.C.: Center for Global Development).

Razafindrakoto, Mireille, and Francois Roubaud. 2010. "Are International Databases on Corruption Reliable? A Comparison of Expert Opinion Surveys and Household Surveys in Sub-Saharan Africa." *World Development* 38, no. 8 (August), pp. 1057–69.

Reinikka, Ritva, and Jakob Svensson. 2002. "Explaining Leakage of Public Funds," Discussion Paper 3227 (London: Centre for Economic Policy Research).

Results for Development Institute. 2015. "Bringing Learning to Light: The Role of Citizen-Led Assessments in Shifting the Education Agenda" (Menlo Park, Calif.: Hewlett Foundation).

Rijkers, Bob, Caroline Freund, and Antonio Nucifora. 2014. "All in the Family: State Capture in Tunisia," Policy Research Working Paper 6810 (Washington, D.C.: World Bank).

Roca, Thomas. 2011. "Measuring Corruption: Perception Surveys or Victimization Surveys? Towards a Better Comprehension of Populations' Perception Mechanisms: Press Freedom, Confidence and Gossip." *SSRN Electronic Journal*, August 15 (https://papers.ssrn.com/sol3/papers2.cfm?abstract_id=1909860).

Roodman, David. 2007. "The Anarchy of Numbers: Aid, Development, and Cross-Country Empirics." *World Bank Economic Review* 21, no. 2 (May), pp. 255–77.

Rose, Richard. 2015. "Reducing Bribery for Public Services Delivered to Citizens," *U4 Brief* 2015:11 (Bergen, Norway: Chr. Michelsen Institute).

Rossotto, Carlo Maria, and others. 2004. "Competition in International

Voice Communications," Working Paper 32526 42 (Washington, D.C.: World Bank).

Sandefur, Justin. 2013. "Here's the Best Thing the U.S. Has Done in Afghanistan." *The Atlantic,* October 10.

Sanyal, Rajib, and Subarna Samanta. 2011. "Trends in International Bribe-Giving: Do Anti-Bribery Laws Matter?" *Journal of International Trade Law and Policy* 10, no. 2, pp. 151–64.

Savedoff, William. 2016. "Anti-Corruption Strategies in Foreign Aid: From Controls to Results," Policy Paper 76 (Washington, D.C.: Center for Global Development).

Shah, Anwar, and Mark Schacter. 2004. "Combating Corruption: Look Before You Leap." *Finance and Development* 41, no. 4 (December), pp. 40–43.

Siegel, Marc. 2005. *False Alarm: The Truth about the Epidemic of Fear* (Hoboken, N.J.: Wiley).

Simone, Francesco de, and Nils Taxell. 2014. "Donors and 'Zero Tolerance for Corruption': From Principle to Practice," *U4 Brief* 2014:2 (Bergen, Norway: Chr. Michelsen Institute).

Skelly, Jenny, Ruth Chalisey, and Paul Pierson. 2010. "Public Attitudes towards Development" (London: UK Department for International Development).

Smith, Emily. 2011. "Controversial Tear Gas Canisters Made in the USA." CNN, January 28 (www.cnn.com/2011/WORLD/africa/01/28/egypt.us.tear.gas/).

Soraya, George. 2009. "Risk Mitigation of Leakage in UPP." Presentation to the World Bank GAC in Projects Group, Washington, D.C, April 21.

Søreide, Tina. 2006. "Procurement Procedures and the Size of Firms in Infrastructure Contracts." Paper prepared for the World Bank Annual Conference on Development Economics, Tokyo, May 29–30.

———. 2009. "Too Risk Averse to Stay Honest? Business Corruption, Uncertainty and Attitudes toward Risk." *International Review of Law and Economics* 29 no. 4 (December), pp. 388–95.

———. 2014. *Drivers of Corruption: A Brief Review* (Washington, D.C.: World Bank).

Søreide, Tina, Linda Gröning, and Rasmus Wandall. 2016. "An Efficient Anticorruption Sanctions Regime? The Case of the World Bank." *Chicago Journal of International Law* 16, no. 2 (January), pp. 523–52.

Søreide, Tina, Arne Tostensen, and Ingvild Aagedal Skage. 2012. *Hunting for Per Diem: The Uses and Abuses of Travel Compensation in Three*

Developing Countries (Oslo: Norwegian Agency for Development Co-operation (Norad)).

Svensson, Jakob. 2005. "Eight Questions about Corruption." *Journal of Economic Perspectives* 19, no. 3 (Summer), pp. 19–42.

Tanzi, Vito, and Hamid Davoodi. 1998. "Roads to Nowhere: How Corruption in Public Investment Hurts Growth," *IMF Economic Issues* 12 (Washington, D.C.: IMF).

Thomas, Melissa A. 2009. "What Do the Worldwide Governance Indicators Measure?" *European Journal of Development Research* 22, no. 1 (February), pp. 31–54.

Times of India. 2015. "India's LPG Cash Subsidy in Bank A/C among Largest Cash Transfer Schemes in World," February 5 (http://timesofindia. indiatimes.com/business/india-business/Indias-LPG-cash-subsidy-in-bank-a/c-among-largest-cash-transfer-schemes-in-world/article-show/46131775.cms).

Tran, Anh. 2008. "Can Procurement Auctions Reduce Corruption: Evidence from the Internal Records of a Bribe-Paying Firm." Job-market paper submitted to the Harvard Kennedy School.

Transparency International. 2015. *People and Corruption: Africa Survey 2015* (Berlin).

TNS Opinion & Social. 2014. "Special Eurobarometer 397: Corruption" (Brussels: European Commission).

Ugur, Mehmet, and Nandini Dasgupta. 2011. *Evidence on the Economic Growth Impacts of Corruption in Low-Income Countries and Beyond: A Systematic Review* (London: EPPI-Centre, Social Science Research Unit, Institute of Education, University of London).

Verspagen, Bart. 2012. "Stylized Facts of Governance, Institutions and Economic Development: Exploring the Institutional Profiles Database," MERIT Working Paper 36 (Maastricht: United Nations University–Maastricht Economic and Social Research Institute on Innovation and Technology).

Walton, Grant, and Sarah Dix. 2013. *Papua New Guinean Understandings of Corruption* (Port Moresby, Papua New Guinea: Transparency International).

Woodhead, Martin, Melanie Frost, and Zoe James. 2013. "Does Growth in Private Schooling Contribute to Education for All? Evidence from a Longitudinal, Two Cohort Study in Andhra Pradesh, India." *Inter-*

national Journal of Educational Development 33, no. 1 (January), pp. 65–73.

World Bank. 2004a. *Annual Review of Development Effectiveness.* Washington, D.C.

———. 2004b. *Improving Investment Climates: An Evaluation of World Bank Group Assistance. Overview Report.* Washington, D.C.

———. 2005. *Capacity Building in Africa: An OED Evaluation of World Bank Support.* Washington, D.C.

———. 2006. *Infrastructure at the Crossroads: Lessons from 20 Years of World Bank Experience.* Washington, D.C.

Index

Absenteeism, 6, 85, 100
Accountability. *See* Voice and accountability
Acemoglu, Daron, 48, 58–59, 65, 67, 88
Afghanistan: Ministry of Public Health accounting standards, 1–2, 12, 96; ODA as percentage of government spending, 94; Open Contracting Data Standard, 104; USAID program to provide basic health care, 1–2, 12
Africa: American survey on effectiveness of foreign aid to, 107; average income levels (1960–2010), 63; firm surveys of corruption, 31; foreign aid, role of, 15; French Research Institute for Development study (2006), 27; leakage of funds designated for education purposes, 5; precolonial ethnic groups and current income levels, 58; UK review on image of

developing countries, 10. *See also individual countries*
Agricultural research and technologies, 105
Aid agencies and programs, 11–15; aid fatigue, 3, 10, 107; corruption investigations, 89; Paris Principles and, 13; receipt-tracking vs. results-tracking, 13, 16; supportive role, 110. *See also* Anticorruption approaches; Policymaking for donors; *specific agencies*
Alatas, Vivi, 50
Ali, Ben, 9
Altruism, 107
Andhra Pradesh, India: absenteeism of government employees, 6; electrical distribution audits, 79; voucher schools and educational outcomes, 77
Andrews, Matt, 98, 99
Anti-Bribery Convention (OECD 1997), 2, 105

Center
for Global
Development

The Center for Global Development works to reduce global poverty and inequality through rigorous research and active engagement with the policy community to make the world a more prosperous, just, and safe place for us all.

The policies and practices of the rich and the powerful—in rich nations, as well as in the emerging powers, international institutions, and global corporations—have significant impacts on the world's poor people. We aim to improve these policies and practices through research and policy engagement to expand opportunities, reduce inequalities, and improve lives everywhere. By pairing research with action, CGD goes beyond contributing to knowledge about development. We conceive of and encourage discussion about practical policy innovations in areas such as trade, aid, health, education, climate change, labor mobility, private investment, access to finance, and global governance to foster shared prosperity in an increasingly interdependent world.

As a nimble, independent, nonpartisan, and nonprofit think tank, we leverage modest resources to combine world-class scholarly research with policy analysis and innovative outreach and communications to turn ideas into action.